Body Matters

**A BIBLICAL UNDERSTANDING OF THE BODY
AND WHY IT MATTERS IN AN AGE OF DISCONTENT**

CHRYSTIE COLE

AMBASSADOR INTERNATIONAL
GREENVILLE, SOUTH CAROLINA & BELFAST, NORTHERN IRELAND

www.ambassador-international.com

Body Matters

ISBN: 978-1-62020-516-7
eISBN: 978-1-62020-423-8

Cover Design & Page Layout by Hannah Nichols
eBook Conversion by Anna Raats

AMBASSADOR INTERNATIONAL
Emerald House
427 Wade Hampton Blvd.
Greenville, SC 29609, USA
www.ambassador-international.com

AMBASSADOR BOOKS
The Mount
2 Woodstock Link
Belfast, BT6 8DD, Northern Ireland, UK
www.ambassadormedia.co.uk

The colophon is a trademark of Ambassador

ACKNOWLEDGEMENTS

As with all Ezer studies, this book is the culmination of the hard work and dedication of many people. First and foremost, this study would not exist without the countless hours of study, research, and wisdom contributed by Bill White and Virginia Griffin.

Thank you to Ella Walker Henderson, Amanda Banks, Dr. Melanie Greene, Wendy Arnold, Elizabeth Middleton, Julie Edwards, Ashlyn Ours, Ashley Stipes, and Jeanette Odom for the time, knowledge, and experiences you generously shared with me during initial meetings. Thank you also to those who took our surveys and to the many women who attended our focus groups in the developmental stages of this study. Your honesty, vulnerability, wisdom, and experience are invaluable and helped shape much of the framework of this study.

To our Pastoral Advisory Team—Bill White, Chris Curtis, Jim Taylor, and Mike Chibbaro—your unapologetic commitment to the Scriptures, wisdom, insight, direction, constructive feedback, encouragement, and partnership are invaluable resources that undergird every Ezer study.

Thank you to our faithful test readers: Meeghan Sowinski, Molly Burns, Ashley Stipes, Meredith Hamby, Alicia Mathers, Libby Thomas,

Julie Edwards, Kelly Swift, Amy Kennedy, Julia Taylor, Carolyn Mayer Berg, Gretchen Dobbs, Susan Jenkins, Mia Huffman, Shannon Griffith, Sherry (and Kenny) Gilliland, Corie Culp, Heather Nelson, Keeley Morrell, Jane Motsinger, Susan Bates, Ashlyn Ours, Lauren Foster, Trina Thiry, Laura Borck, Amanda O'Kelly, Tonia Hawkinson, Sara Fowler, Megan Gaminde, Laura Baxley, and Carol Black. You gave of your time and energy to provide distinct perspectives and constructive critique, and many of your words can be found on these pages.

I am deeply indebted to the prayer team who covered this project in prayer and who faithfully and fervently prayed for the women who will read the contents of these pages: Lauren Nelson, Shari Horner, Ginger Kumler, Rose Marshall, Jamie Adams, Keri Geary, Renee Sweeny, Susanna Johnson, Joyce Leftwich, Catie Chance, Narissa Materra, Renee DeMoss, Cindy Chibbaro, Cindy Barwick, Karen Swoap, Libby Thomas, Kara Orr, and Kristin Ellis. Thank you for your heart for this project and for constantly placing it before the Lord in prayer.

Thank you to our incredible communications team: Scott Mozingo, Tish Pitman, Abby Moore, and Matt New for your creative insights, attention to detail, and commitment to excellence.

And finally, thank you to all the women of Grace Church who prayed for the Body Matters conference and its attendees, the countless women who shared experiences, attended the conference, participated in the Body Matters Institute Classes, and provided feedback on the beginning stages of this study. This study is the fruit of your contributions, and we are forever grateful for your time, energy, and resources.

CONTENTS

1

THE BODY MATTERS

Fat. Saggy. Dissatisfied. Frumpy. Mediocre. Ugly. Dumpy. Disgusted. Tired. Aging. Blah. Plump. Frustrated. Coping. Trapped. It is what it is. Discouraged.

As a woman, it's not difficult to look at this list of words and figure out what they are describing. In fact, we have probably even used a few of these same words ourselves. A couple of years ago, we surveyed three hundred women from our church about their bodies, and these are the real words they chose to describe them. My personal favorite is the woman who described her body as *lush*. I can almost picture it.

I've had my own issues with my body since I was a teenager, and I knew I wasn't alone. But seeing those surveys made the issue that much more real to me. My heart sunk as I thought about these women whom the Lord loves with an everlasting love, those whom He fashioned intimately within their mothers' wombs. Through reading those surveys, my eyes were opened to the depth of brokenness, despair, frustration, and bondage so many women are in when it comes to their own bodies.

More than ninety-five percent of the responses were negative, even dismal. And the remaining five percent weren't much better: patient, tolerant, optimistic, a work in progress, hopeful. Even these responses hint at the underlying *dis*-ease present within many women. Less than one percent of respondents actually gave a positive response. When asked what part of their body they dislike the most, everything from head to toe was covered: hair, eyes, complexion, teeth, smile, ears, nose, neck, cuticles, arms, hips, legs, feet, height, weight, wrinkles, thighs, ankles, and stomach. Seventy-eight percent confessed that they feel more confident when they feel attractive. Sixty-two percent believed that they would be happier if they were thinner. Ninety-seven percent declared they are conscious of what they eat on a daily basis. Fifty-nine percent of the women confessed that they almost *regularly* compare themselves to other women, with thirty-three percent stating they *sometimes* compare themselves. Less than one percent said they *never* compare themselves.[1]

The women surveyed, ranging in age from their teens to their sixties, represent a diverse group of women. They are young women who are coming of age in an airbrushed and hyper-sexualized society, young mothers grappling with their post-baby bodies, middle-aged women who are seeing the effects of gravity and aging, and older women who are experiencing the reality of a body that is losing its functionality. They represent physically healthy women as well as those struggling with chronic pain, illness, and disabilities. They represent women who engage in regular physical activity and those who don't, women who have struggled with eating disorders and women who haven't. They are women who feel inadequate because of their thin frames and women who feel inadequate because of their ample frames.

While this is a diverse group of women, they all share one commonality: an underlying discomfort in their own skin and a desire to measure up to a standard—whether their own personal expectations or those imposed on them by society. And this goes beyond mere body and body image issues. For a woman, her image is often embodied in everything she portrays to a watching world—her appearance, her home, her children, her husband, her job, her schooling, her accomplishments, and of course, her body.

The inability to be comfortable in her skin manifests itself in different ways in different women. Some women may find it hard to genuinely engage other women whom they find prettier, fitter, or better dressed. Some may spend inordinate amounts of time and money attempting to craft the perfect image through diet, exercise, clothing, and cosmetics. Still more may experience the pangs of inferiority, insecurity, envy, and jealousy. Some may be hypersensitive about certain aspects of their bodies, like their post-baby bellies, and have trouble engaging in physical intimacy with their husbands. Other women may avoid social gatherings that require a swimsuit and may even avoid exercising around others for fear of being judged.

Though many women have at least one aspect of their body they are frustrated with, not every woman struggles with discontentment and despair. Some women may be content with their bodies and have not had to work through body-related issues yet. For these women, it may be hard to be compassionate and to relate to the feelings of inadequacy other women have toward their bodies. Instead of frustration or despair regarding their bodies, they feel a sense of personal pride and judgment toward those who "don't take care of themselves" or who don't exercise self-control. Or they may find themselves on the receiving end of judgment when women who see their naturally lean build roll their eyes and say, "I wish I had your problem." A woman who is athletically inclined may feel proud of the way her body performs. Perhaps some women even use their bodies as a way to gain affirmation and overcome insecurities in other areas of their lives.

At some point in time, we will all face issues of aging or disease that will impact the form (appearance) and the functionality (performance) of our bodies. **Regardless of your current feelings about your body—whether content, proud, or discouraged—you cannot afford to place your confidence in your body in form or in functionality because both will fade and one day fail you.** It is important to approach this topic with an open mind because the manifestations of body-related issues are more insidious and systemic than we may currently recognize.

Questions for Reflection

1. What three words would you use to describe your body?

2. What three words would you use to describe the bodies of some of your friends?

3. Are your descriptions of yourself better or worse than your descriptions of your friends? Why? Discuss as a group.

4. How do you receive compliments from others? Is your response different when receiving compliments on appearance versus compliments on your character? What kind of compliments do you value most?

5. Do you identify as more content with your body or more frustrated? Why?

6. Which aspect of your body do you struggle with most—the form (appearance) or functionality (performance)?

HUMBLE DEPENDENCE

When I first began studying this topic, I thought I knew the answers I would find. But what I didn't realize is that I was approaching this topic with my own preconceived ideas and solutions, and I thought Scripture would confirm my opinions. But over time, the Lord revealed my arrogance and exposed the sin within my own heart. The issue of body and body image is complex. It is not as easy as covering up your mirror or accepting yourself as you are, and we need to resist the temptation to prescribe either overly simplistic or overly rigid solutions.

A topic of this nature requires an open mind and a spirit of humility. It is possible that what we have thought and practiced over the years may not actually be true. Scripture must be our guide and our foundation if we hope to find clarity and freedom. Though the Bible doesn't provide much specific direction regarding diet, exercise, and general self-care, it does have plenty to say about how a woman who follows Christ should think, feel, and act toward her body. God has given us everything we need for living a godly life (2 Peter 1:3). Therefore, we will approach the Scripture with humble dependence and confidence as we seek clarity through the Holy Spirit and biblical community regarding what our bodies mean to the Lord and how we should care for them in response.

Throughout this study, we will submit ourselves to Scripture, not make Scripture submit to us. It is important to resist the temptation to say more than Scripture on this subject. This may frustrate those of us who want a quick-fix or simple formula, because it leaves us in a position of tension where we have to seek the Lord through Scripture, the Holy Spirit, and biblical community regarding what it looks like to be faithful stewards of our bodies. This does not mean that science, society, culture, and doctors have nothing of value to offer us. On the contrary, God is at work in this world, through believers and unbelievers, for the good of the earth. He uses the advancements of science, the wisdom of the culture, and the knowledge we have gained through study of the body to aid us in tending to the needs of all mankind. Therefore, we can recognize that science and doctors may have much to say on this and many other topics. Our job is to take what we learn from them and examine it by God's Word—holding it up to the light of his truth and allowing Scripture to determine whether a thing is true, wise, prudent, good for us, good for others, and glorifying to God.

CULTURAL IMPACT

Women in the western culture are inundated with media's portrayal of ideal bodies—whether it's tall and lean or voluptuous and sexy. In his documentary *America the Beautiful,* Darryl Roberts estimated that the average teenager is exposed to 3.3 hours of magazines, 7.6 hours of Internet, and 10.6 hours of television per week.[2] These carefully constructed images persuade us to buy into the lie displayed on the cover of every magazine, billboard, television, and movie screen. And with the introduction of social media, it is easier than ever to compare yourself to women all over the world. No matter how vigilant you are to protect yourself from the unrealistic ideals portrayed, they are inescapable.

We are responsible for how we respond to these images, but we cannot deny the impact they have over time and ongoing exposure. Roberts cited a case conducted in Fiji by Harvard sociologist Dr. Anne Becker. Becker visited Fiji in 1982 before western television had been introduced and found that a larger body was the valued standard for women at that time. A larger woman indicated strength, health, and ability, which was highly important in that society. *Her body reflected the needs of the community.* But when western television shows, such as Melrose Place and Beverly Hills 90210, were introduced in 1995, all of that began to change. After three years of exposure to these programs, eleven percent of young girls admitted to vomiting to control their weight, teen drug use and pregnancy were on the rise, and a general disrespect of authority had increased as well. Becker concluded that in just three short years, centuries of cultural traditions had been undone.

While this issue is pervasive in our western society, there are standards of beauty that govern every culture. In countries like India, Thailand, and some parts of Africa, having lighter skin is associated with affluence and has caused a surge in the skin-lightening cream industry. In Mauritania, there are fat-farms, not to slim women down but to fatten them up, because larger women are considered more attractive.[3] In South Korea, more women are having plastic surgery to widen their eyes, making them appear more western. In Ethiopia, young girls are cut over and over again in order to develop scars in intricate patterns in order to attract a husband. And in Iran, bandages from nose jobs are sported as badges of honor as the women embark on the ultimate quest for beauty and affluence.[4]

It is plain to see that, all over the world, a woman's quest for image, beauty, significance, and approval comes at great cost. But this doesn't even begin to take into account the numbers of women who suffer from disordered eating like anorexia and bulimia, those who are morbidly obese, the millions undergoing countless elective procedures to alter their appearance, those enslaved to their gym routines and diet regimens, the women frantically searching for the right formulas and anti-aging creams, women who self-medicate through food, and those who silently suffer general feelings of discontent and inadequacy.

There is no lack of advice and prescriptions within our world today. If you have a problem, someone has a solution, something to say, a promise to offer, or a product to sell you. Everyone believes they have the right diet, the right form of exercise, the right pill. Fad diets and new trends in exercise are a dime a dozen. The messages of our society are loud and clear: you need to lose weight, shape up, erase the signs of aging and wrinkles on your face, and develop rock-hard abs. *We are so disoriented by the multitude of messages bombarding us that it is hard to know how to define a healthy body and body image.*

Two dominant voices speaking into this topic are pop culture and religious culture. Mainstream culture often has an obsessive perspective toward the body, while many faith-based cultures marginalize the importance of the body, focusing on "higher" matters of the soul. While both may have positive contributions to make, by themselves they offer incomplete and conflicting views that leave women struggling to find freedom in this area of their lives. Below are some of the more common ideas present within each:

Messages in Pop Culture	Messages in Religious Culture
"Thin is in"	The body isn't important, doesn't matter
"Strong is the new skinny"	Taking care of your body is selfish
"Real women have curves"	A woman's body entices a man to sin
Perfection is the goal/standard	The inner person is all that matters
Perfection is achievable	Focus on outward appearance is vanity
You are entitled to beauty	Beauty is irrelevant/should be rejected
The body is elevated to exclusion of soul	The soul is elevated to exclusion of body
How you look determines your value	How you look determines your spirituality (e.g., a healthy person is more spiritual; a modest/frumpy person is more spiritual)
Fitness and diet will prolong your life	The body isn't meant to be preserved
Youth is more valued	Wisdom is more valued

Looking at these conflicting messages, it is obvious why we have so much trouble navigating this area of our lives. The messages we hear on a regular basis are contradictory at best and disorienting at worst. This makes it a challenge for a woman who follows Christ to know how she should think about, care for, and feel about her body. We could continue to put forth overly simplistic, self-help ideologies like self-acceptance and self-affirmation. We could respond to the cultural ideals of beauty by boycotting, lobbying, and taking an in-your-face approach, touting that others need to appreciate us just as we are. Or we could settle into a victim mentality, believing we are just the unfortunate recipients of bad genes or stuck in a society that overly emphasizes physical beauty. *But all of these solutions will fall far short of the real, abiding peace and freedom available to us as Christians.*

GETTING CLEAR BEFORE WE MOVE ON

Before we go further, we must address a couple of issues. If you are like me, it is entirely possible that you are also bringing in pre-conceived ideas/beliefs on what's right, what's good, what's wrong, what's better regarding your body, and how you should take care of it. Or perhaps you have unrealistic expectations and are coming in looking for a fix that no study can provide you. Similarly, we all have baggage and real wounds in this area. Many women have been shaped by behavior and attitudes that were modeled by our mothers, grand-mothers, cousins, friends, or other significant women. Probably just as many have been affected by our fathers and other significant male figures. Some women still bear the scars from the thoughtless and unkind words of others. Whatever names you were called, whatever hurtful things were said to you, these words helped shape how you view yourself today. This baggage and these wounds cause many women to self-protect or self-promote in a way that can make it virtually impossible for others to speak into their lives regarding their bodies. So before we move on, it is important to take some time to reflect on the following questions:

What hurts and insecurities are you bringing into this study?

How might past wounds be blinding you to your own sin in this area?

What preconceived ideas about the body and care of the body are you bringing into this study?

In what ways are you currently enslaved in your own sin and paralyzed from moving toward help and healing?

What expectations do you have from this study? Are they realistic expectations?

In what ways do you hope to grow in knowledge, understanding, and practice where your body is concerned?

Over the coming weeks, commit these things to prayer. Instead of asking the Lord to fill your desires and meet your expectations, ask him to transform your desires so that they match his desires for you. Likewise, take your hurts and insecurities to the Lord and ask Him to bring the healing and comfort you need in order to move on and grow.

WHY A STUDY ON THE BODY?

The author of Hebrews said we should "throw off every weight that slows us down, especially the sin that so easily trips us up" that we might run the race of faith with endurance (Hebrews 12:1 NLT). A life of faith requires endurance. We won't be able to endure well as followers of Christ with sin and baggage entangling us. Both despair and pride about her body will weigh a woman down, distract her from the goal, and hinder her from moving forward in faith and obedience to the Lord and service to others. **As a Christian woman, how you think about and care for your body is an issue of discipleship and growth in spiritual maturity.** It is important to note here, though, that how you care for your body has nothing to do with God's love for and acceptance of you. *You are saved by grace through faith in Jesus Christ alone.*

> God saved you by his grace when you believed. And you can't take credit for this; it is a gift from God. Salvation is not a reward for the good things we have done, so none of us can boast about it. For we are God's masterpiece. He has created us anew in Christ Jesus so we can do the good things he planned for us long ago.
>
> ~ Ephesians 2:8–10 NLT

How you feel about and care or don't care for your body has no bearing on who you are in Christ. You are fully accepted by God because of Christ's righteousness, not based on your own performance. But how you feel about and care or don't care for your body can determine the measure of joy you experience in this life as well as hin-

der your growth in spiritual maturity and your effectiveness for the ⌉
kingdom of God. ⌋

The book of Proverbs rightly warns us that "there is a path before each person that seems right, but it ends in death" (Proverbs 14:12 NLT). The topic of our bodies is a sensitive and deeply personal one, but it is one we must address. If we are to find real freedom and hope, then we must be willing to have our own sin, idolatry, weaknesses, and preconceived ideas exposed. The real problem is not how we look, how much we weigh, whether we are young or old, tall or short, big-boned or petite. *The real issue is sin and the distinctive way it manifests itself in the life of a woman and how she looks to Christ to free her from captivity to that sin.* Our goal is not about identifying a specific health or fitness solution. **The goal of this study is to help us learn why the body matters to the Lord and how we should care for the bodies He has entrusted to us in order that we may fulfill His purposes.**

Therefore, let us approach this study as the Psalmsist who prayed, "Search me, O God, and know my heart; test me and know my anxious thoughts. Point out anything in me that offends you, and lead me along the path of everlasting life" (Psalms 139:23–24 NLT).

Questions for Reflection

1.   In the Fiji study, Dr. Becker found that the valued standard for the Fijian woman's body reflected the needs of her community. Does the western ideal for a woman's body reflect the needs of the community? Why or why not? Discuss as a group.

2.   How aware are you of your body or appearance? How often does it cross your mind?

3.   How would you define beauty? Discuss as a group.

4.   What do you hope to gain through this study?

THE TRUTH OF THE BODY

Driving at night is a challenge for me. I am easily disoriented when the light of day gives way to darkness, especially on backcountry roads near my home. It makes it hard to figure out where I am in order to get where I am going. And the darkness is deceptive, casting shadows of things I think are real but aren't. I wonder if the same might be true for us where our bodies are concerned. Have we been under the cover of night for so long that we have become disoriented and lost our way?

The darkness surrounding body and body image is thick in our current culture, and I believe many of us have become disoriented and lost. Some women attempting to navigate the confusion veer off course by magnifying the body, treating it as an end instead of a means—as an object to be displayed or used for self-gratifying purposes. Others drift toward denigrating the body, devaluing it to the point of abuse or neglect. While still others swing between extremes, experiencing seasons of frenetic activity followed by seasons of apathetic passivity. But none of these bring us any closer to our destination—freedom from the tyranny of self. We need a robust biblical understanding that can shed light on our idolatry of and ignorance toward our bodies.

TOWARD A BIBLICAL UNDERSTANDING OF THE BODY

You are more than just a body. You are also more than just a soul. The body and soul are intertwined, making up the whole of who you are as a person. You cannot separate one from another. Your physical body is tied to your spiritual life. What affects one may, over time, affect the other. For example, ongoing stress may lead to high blood pressure, depression, sleep deprivation, or ulcers. Similarly, chronic pain or extreme fatigue may eventually affect your personal joy and peace, or your relationship with God and others. Your body and soul are inextricably linked.

Scripture addresses the whole person, body and soul. We see this clearly throughout Jesus' ministry as the healing of the body is closely connected to the person's faith and the forgiveness of sins (Luke 5:17–26, Matthew 9:18–26, Matthew 15:21–31). Jesus spent much of His time healing and preaching. He addressed the needs of the *whole* person. He tended to the bodies of men and women. He fed them, washed them, and cared for them. He healed them all—the lame, the blind, the sick—and He raised the dead. And He did all of this while caring for their souls—teaching in the synagogues, proclaiming the good news of the kingdom, the forgiveness of sins, and the hope of restoration of humanity to a right relationship with God (Matthew 4:23). Furthermore, Jesus tells us that the greatest commandment is to love the Lord with all your heart, soul, mind, and strength and to love your neighbor as yourself. This is what it means to be disciples of Christ, and this cannot be accomplished apart from your body.

The point of all of this is that the body is a spiritual matter of utmost importance; *your body matters.* We cannot afford to reject, neglect, or marginalize the body, nor can we afford to exalt, worship, or idolize the body. The body matters to the Lord, and it matters to His church, so we must gain a biblical understanding of the body and how we are to relate to it in response. This means we need to weed out the lies we believe and build a solid understanding of the body based on God's truth, allowing it to shape how we think, feel, and act regarding our bodies.

LIE #1: IT'S MY BODY.

This is perhaps the most disorienting lie of all, and it manifests itself in various ways in a woman's life. This inaccurate assumption guides many of the decisions we make about how we care for and govern our bodies. A woman who believes this lie may abuse her body through cutting, eating disorders like bulimia and anorexia, or even restrictive diets and extreme exercise regimens. Another woman may neglect her body, ignoring its need for proper rest, nourishment, and regular physical activity. While another woman may treat her body as a self-improvement project, carefully constructing her physical image by subjecting it to cosmetic surgeries and shaping and toning muscle groups. Others indulge the body, gratifying its desires for decadence, food, and alcohol. Regardless of the way this lie manifests itself in the life of a woman, the fundamental belief is the same: My body belongs to me and it is mine to do with as I please.

And this belief will more often than not impair a woman's ability to make wise decisions in caring for her body. So what is the truth?

TRUTH: YOU WERE CREATED BY GOD AND FOR GOD.

The very beginning chapters of Scripture tell the story of the creation of the first man and woman. In Genesis 1, the Lord forms all the beasts of the land, sky, and sea. He forms the heavens and the earth, the sun, the moon, and the stars. He sets all things in their place and gives them a role to play – the sun giving light to the day and the moon to the night, the creatures to be fruitful and multiply and fill the earth, and the seed-bearing plants to spread their seed and fill the earth with vegetation. Then on the sixth day, God determines to create the first man and woman:

> Then God said, "Let us make human beings in our image, to be like us. They will reign over the fish in the sea, the birds in the sky, the livestock, all the wild animals on the earth, and the small animals that scurry along the ground."
>
> So God created human beings in his own image. In the image of God he created them; male and female he created them.
>
> Then God blessed them and said, "Be fruitful and multiply. Fill the earth and govern it. Reign over the fish in the sea, the birds in the sky, and all the animals that scurry along the ground."
>
> ~ Genesis 1:26–28 NLT

We were created *by* God. He formed and fashioned each of us in our mother's womb, making all the delicate, inner parts of our bodies (Psalms 139). Our existence is not a random occurrence without rhyme or reason, but the intentional, deliberate action by the same powerful God who existed before anything else—the one who created the heavens and earth and everything in them, and who holds all of creation together by His power (Colossians 1:17).

But this is only one important aspect of our creation. We gain a second insight in Paul's letter to the Corinthian church as he addresses the sexual immorality present within the church:

> You can't say that our bodies were made for sexual immorality. They were made for the Lord, and the Lord cares about our bodies.
>
> ~ 1 Corinthians 6:13b NLT

Paul reiterates this in the book of Colossians when he declares that *all* things were created by him and for him (Colossians 1:16). We were not only created *by* God; we were also created *for* God. It is likely we know this to some degree, but perhaps we have never taken time to really consider what this means to our daily lives. It is easy to be deceived into believing that we have ownership over our own bodies. But the reality is we do not belong to ourselves; we belong to the Lord. He made us *for* Himself, and this has significant implications for how we live.

If we were created by God and for God, then there must be some purpose or intent behind our creation, some reason the Lord called us into being. Going back to the first chapter in Genesis, we find some clarity into God's rationale. We were created to reflect His image and to be like Him (v. 26), to work—to rule and to reign (vv. 26, 28), to govern the earth (v. 28), and to be fruitful and multiply—filling the earth with other image bearers (v. 28).

More specifically, in the second chapter of Genesis we see that God created the woman with a special purpose, one that is a common call to all women for all times. He created women to be an *ezer-kenegdo,* an essential counterpart, one who comes alongside another in the context of relationship in order to bring strength and life in a way that empowers that person to do and be something they could not otherwise do and be (Genesis 2:18, 20).[1]

The book of Isaiah also gives us insight into our reason for existence as God declares, "Bring all who claim me as their God, *for I have made them for my glory.* It was I who created them" (Isaiah 43:7 NLT, emphasis mine). Furthermore, in the New Testament the Apostle Paul declares that we were created to be instruments for God's special purposes and to do the good works He planned for us long ago (2 Timothy 2:21, Ephesians 2:10). **Our bodies are not just our own outward personal expression to the world; they are instruments God intends to use to accomplish His purposes and to bring Him glory.**

Somewhere along the way, we began to use our bodies to gain our own glory, satisfy our own desires, and fulfill our own purposes. To seek praise and glory through your physical appearance or to use your body to serve your own agenda is to live contrary to God's intended purposes. When we struggle to see how our bodies are relevant to our spiritual maturity, we are prone to indulge or neglect them, to exalt or despise them. The point is that far too often our thoughts regarding our bodies do not align with God's:

God created people with bodies, and God declared that they were good. It is sometimes hard for us modern-day Christians to grasp that central fact. Bodies are not simply pieces of furniture to decorate or display; they are not trappings about which we have conflicted feelings ('body images' that we need to revamp or retool); they are not objects to be dieted away, made to conform to popular standards or made to perform unthinkable athletic feats with the help of drugs; they are neither tools for scoring points nor burdens to overcome. They are simply good.[2]   *my body is good.*

The implications of this are too great to overlook. Our bodies were created by God and for God. And at the end of the creation account in Genesis 1, God looks over all of his creation, including our bodies, and declares it exceedingly, abundantly *beautiful!*[3]

Following Jesus with regard to your body and growing as a mature disciple begins by acknowledging His ownership over your body and its goodness as one of God's beautiful creations. If you were created by God and for God, then your perception and treatment of your body is an issue of discipleship; it is an issue of *bringing everything you do to and with your body under the authority of the Lord.* The beautiful and comforting truth is that your body matters to the Lord, and He has entrusted it to you to care for it in His best interest.

At the end of the creation story in Genesis 2, the Lord looks over all He has created and declares it very good. He places the first man and woman in the Garden to enjoy and tend to His creation. They are in perfect harmony with God, with each other, and with themselves. They are surrounded by the abundance and flourishing of God's good creation. Death, suffering, loss, illness, and pain are not a part of their current reality.

But all of that changes when they step out from under God's protective covering and choose their own way instead. Rather than acknowledging the Lord's ownership, Adam and Eve commit the ultimate treason; they use the same body God entrusted to them to rebel against Him. As a result of their rebellion, they bring the curse of sin, death, and suffering onto the entire creation (Romans 5:12–17). This brings us to the second lie.

Questions for Reflection

1. Do you tend to act more like an owner or a manager (steward) of your body? How?

2. What do your actions communicate more: that you believe you were created for God or that you believe He was created for you?

3. Have you ever spent time reflecting on the truth that God was intimately involved in forming and fashioning you exactly as you are? How could that truth change the way you think about and act toward your body?

LIE #2: I CAN REVERSE THE CURSE.

At first glance, this might seem to be a ridiculous idea. Not many women would openly admit that they believe they can reverse the curse, but how we live often reveals our true beliefs. This insidious lie is difficult to uncover because it is often concealed underneath the ruse of "healthy living." This has enslaved some women to excessive, even obsessive standards for food. Every time a food is potentially linked to disease, it is cut from the list of acceptable foods to eat. Rigid dietary restrictions dictate their lives and the lives of their families. **Our choices should be guided by wisdom, not obsession and fear.** There may be times when any one of these choices is appropriate. Many suffer from food allergies that require them to eliminate certain foods from their diet. Other times new information becomes available, like how smoking causes cancer and lung disease, which helps us make wise choices in how we care for our bodies. But far too often these choices are made out of fear and an attempt to control the future. It's evidenced in a woman's endless striving toward perfection and attempts to stave off the inevitable. For other women it may manifest itself through spending inordinate amounts of money on cosmetic surgeries, anti-aging creams, or covering all traces of gray in an attempt to avoid the reality of aging. Or believing that if you work your body long enough and hard enough through strenuous exercise and "healthy" eating, you are *guaranteed* a long, healthy life. At the root of many of these actions is the desire to be in control of our own bodies. We want to resist disease, aging, and death because it is not as it should be. We are responsible to make wise choices in self-care, but we will not avoid the curse.

TRUTH: THE BODY IS CORRUPTED.

While our bodies are God's good creation, the reality we know all too well is that our bodies are corrupted. Sin has invaded them, and as a result they are not what God created them to be. They know pain, suffering, sin, and death that they were never intended to know. From the day we are born, we are dying. We face this truth every day as we visit loved ones in the hospital, as we see the marks of time spread across our faces, and as we grapple with disease, with fatigue, and with bodies that no longer function as they once did. Paul says that, as a result of this, all of creation groans, longing for the day when it will be freed from its subjection to death and decay. And we also groan as we long for our bodies to be released from sin and suffering once and for all (Romans 8:18–23).

The corruption of the body and the pain it causes cannot be avoided. We experience it in a variety of ways in different seasons of our life. It may be watching someone you love slowly slip away into the clutches of Alzheimer's or forms of dementia. Or perhaps you've personally struggled with a mental illness like depression or schizophrenia. Some women have bodies that are governed by chronic fatigue or chronic pain like migraines. Or perhaps bearing children is a hope you never got to realize because of infertility. Diseases like multiple sclerosis and Lou Gehrig's disease (ALS) imprison women in their bodies everyday. Cancer, heart attacks, high blood pressure, diabetes, sports-related injuries, and even the common cold are reminders of the frailty of our bodies and our dependence on God for life and breath. We are fragile, dependent. Even those who are strong and healthy now, those who rigorously train their bodies, will not escape the decay of the body that time and age bring.

But God is not ignorant to your suffering. He does not turn a blind eye to your need. God was intimately involved in your creation (Psalms 139). He was there, present with you. He knew from the beginning of time every mental, emotional, physical, and spiritual challenge you would have. He knows you intimately—from the top of your head to the tips of your toes—every nerve ending, every brain cell, every feature of your face, every hair on your head. Nothing you suffer takes Him by surprise—no birth defect, no disability, no disease (Psalms 139:1–16). He is already at work on your behalf. He so loves His creation that He set a plan in motion all the way back in Genesis 3, promising to send one who would crush the head of the serpent (v. 15), thereby conquering sin and death once and for all.

No matter how hard you work, you will not avoid sickness, suffering, aging, or death. But as a believer in Christ, you do not have to live in fear or be enslaved to your attempts to control the outcome because as a Christian, the outcome is already secure. Christ overcame sin, suffering, and death in our place. He is the only one who could reverse the curse and secure our futures. So we do not have to live in fear and insecurity. Instead we can live in anticipation of the day when Christ returns and death is conquered once and for all. And until that day, Paul reminds us that we can rejoice even in our suffering because suffering produces endurance, endurance produces character, and character produces hope (Romans 5:3–4).

Contrary to the hope we place in our physical bodies—in their ability to perform or in their appearance—the hope produced through suffering will not lead to disappointment, "For we know how dearly God loves us, because he has given us the Holy Spirit to fill our hearts with his love" (Romans 5:5b NLT). This leads us to the next lie to uncover about our bodies.

Questions for Reflection

1. If you had to categorize yourself, would you tend more toward "over-obsessing" about your appearance or more toward "not caring" about your appearance? Why?

2. What role does fear and insecurity play in your choices of food, exercise, and other self-care?

3. How have you personally suffered the curse on your body? What is your response to suffering (e.g., avoidance, acceptance, fear, longing)?

LIE #3: MY BODY IS IRRELEVANT TO MY FAITH.

Many women struggle to see how their physical bodies matter to their faith. Living from this inaccurate assumption leads many women to disregard the role their body plays in their spiritual condition. A woman who ignores physical disciplines like proper nutrition and regular physical activity but sets aside time for spiritual disciplines may not understand the important correlation between her bodily life and her spiritual life. Some women may overindulge their bodies through food, alcohol, or laziness. While others may neglect the body's need for nourishment and rest, burning the candle at both ends and never stopping long enough to tend to the needs of the body. Some may pamper the body, and others may treat it harshly. Regardless of the way this faulty belief manifests itself in your life, the reality is that **the life of faith is lived and experienced through your body**. The Lord not only created your body, He has chosen it as His dwelling place, and as His instrument to be used for His good purposes.

TRUTH: YOUR BODY IS A TEMPLE.

Your body is a temple of the Holy Spirit. It is how God currently resides among humanity. This means that your body is of utmost importance to your faith.

In his letter to the Corinthians, Paul affirms the value and importance of the body for a follower of Christ. Paul, rebuking the Corinthian church regarding the sexual immorality among some of its members, says,

> Don't you realize that your bodies are actually parts of Christ? Should a man take his body, which is part of Christ, and join it to a prostitute? Never! And don't you realize that if a man joins himself to a prostitute, he becomes one body with her? For the Scriptures say, "The two are united into one." But the person who is joined to the Lord is one spirit with him.

> Run from sexual sin! No other sin so clearly affects the body as this one does. For sexual immorality is a sin against your own body. Don't you realize that your body is the temple of the Holy Spirit, who lives in you and was given to you by God? You do not belong to yourself, for God bought you with a high price. So you must honor God with your body.

> ~ 1 Corinthians 6:15-20 NLT

In essence, Paul says that there is a mystical union that occurs when a person places their faith in Christ. **If you are a Christian, your physical body is actually part of Christ; you are "one spirit with Him" because the Holy Spirit lives in you.** The indwelling presence of the Holy Spirit within you is a mark of God's ownership of you, and this means that what you do *with* and *to* your body matters.

This truth sometimes gets corrupted and twisted into a spiritualized form of self-glorification. When this is the case, it is sometimes used as justification for exercise and dieting that is less about honoring and serving God and more about honoring ourselves and serving our own agenda. It is also sometimes used to boost our waning self-esteem in order to make us feel better about ourselves. Rather than humbly receiving this truth and directing our focus outward toward the worship of God, we turn inward toward the worship of the embodied self.

The truth that our bodies are temples of the Holy Spirit should not inflate our feelings of superiority or self-importance. Instead, the fact that we are united to Christ in body and a temple for His Spirit should humble us and give us pause to think about how we live, the daily choices we make, and how we honor God with our bodies— including how we think about, feel about, and nurture them. This truth also impacts how we use our bodies. Our bodies are a source of blessing to others, both in the way we give them to our spouses[5] and in the way we serve one another.

But all of that is only one aspect of your body as a temple. While it is true that each woman is, individually, a temple of the Holy Spirit, this is not the main emphasis in Scripture. The majority of the New Testament focuses on the fact that we, corporately, as the church, make up the body of Christ and house His Spirit.

> Don't you realize that all of you **together** are the temple of God and that the Spirit of God lives in you.
>
> ~ 1 Corinthians 3:16 NLT, emphasis mine

Paul reiterates this in his letter to the Ephesians:

> So now you Gentiles are no longer strangers and foreigners. You are citizens along with all of God's holy people. You are members of God's family. **Together**, we are his house, built on the foundation of the apostles and the prophets. And the cornerstone is Christ Jesus himself. We are carefully joined together in him, becoming a holy temple for the Lord. Through him you Gentiles are also being made part of this dwelling where God lives by his Spirit.
>
> ~ Ephesians 2:19–22 NLT, emphasis mine

So the Spirit of God lives in us *individually* and He also lives among us *corporately* in the body of believers that make up His church. This truth has implications for how we live individually as well as corporately. The embodied life is not all about us, and our bodies are not ours to do with as we please. "The body is a temple, the place where God dwells. And the one who dwells in the temple shall act for its welfare: 'the Lord is for the body.'"⁶ **Your body matters to the Lord, and it matters to His church.**

Questions for Reflection

1. Your body is a temple where the Holy Spirit dwells. How should that truth impact your thoughts and actions toward your body?

2. Your body is one part that makes up the whole body of Christ, where the Holy Spirit dwells. How should that truth impact your thoughts and actions toward your body?

3. Have you ever thought about the fact that your body is one small part of a whole?

THE FUTURE OF YOUR BODY

Our current body is perishable and marked by corruption. It is prone to sickness and weariness. It is feeble in mind and body, vulnerable to sinful desires and to temptation. Muscles will weaken, bones will become brittle, hair will gray and fall out, and eyes and ears will begin to fail. This body is deteriorating day by day on a trajectory toward the grave. But by God's grace, death does not have the last word.

> Our earthly bodies are planted in the ground when we die, but they will be raised to live forever. Our bodies are buried in brokenness, but they will be raised in glory. They are buried in weakness, but they will be raised in strength. They are buried as natural human bodies, but they will be raised as spiritual bodies.
>
> ~ 1 Corinthians 15:42b–44a NLT

When Christ returns, each of us will be given a new body, one that is no longer marked by corruption. They will not deteriorate or grow old; they will not be vulnerable to sickness or disease. Rather than be fragile or frail, they will be strong and capable. These new bodies will no longer be vulnerable to sin and temptation. And they will be indestructible, no longer subject to death. The flesh and the spirit will no longer war against one another. Instead, we will finally be whole and able to worship and serve the Lord in a way we've never known. And we will live in peace with ourselves, with God, and with one another forever. This is the lavish inheritance that awaits us as followers of Christ—the free gift of God to all who believe in Jesus as Lord and Savior.

Though this is not our present reality and outwardly our bodies are wasting away, we look forward with hope, knowing that one day they will be resurrected, glorified, and eternal:

> For we know that when this earthly tent we live in is taken down (that is, when we die and leave this earthly body), we will have a house in heaven, an eternal body made for us by God himself and not by human hands. We grow weary in our present bodies, and we long to put on our heavenly bodies like new clothing. For we will put on heavenly bodies; we will not be spirits without bodies. While we live in these earthly bodies, we groan and sigh, but it's not that we want to die and get rid of these bodies that clothe us. Rather, we want to put on our new bodies so that these dying bodies will be swallowed up by life. God himself has prepared us for this, and as a guarantee he has given us his Holy Spirit.

~ 2 Corinthians 5:1–5 NLT

If you are struggling with your body, if you are suffering from major challenges with illness or you are frustrated by your body's limitations, take comfort in the knowledge that what you are now is not what you will be. *Though we will all be buried in weakness and brokenness, we will be raised in power and strength.*

The good news of the gospel applies not just to the salvation of our souls but also to the resurrection of our bodies, for:

> Just as death came into the world through a man, now the resurrection from the dead has begun through another man. Just as everyone dies because we all belong to Adam, everyone who belongs to Christ will be given new life. But there is an order to this resurrection: Christ was raised as the first of the harvest; then all who belong to Christ will be raised when he comes back.
>
> ~ 1 Corinthians 15:21-23 NLT

Though pain, death, and suffering came into the world through the sin of Adam, God did not allow it to end there. In His great mercy, He sent Jesus Christ in human form—*in a body*—to atone or pay for the sins of humanity. He did this so that all who believe in Jesus would be made right with God through faith, adopted into the family of God, made co-heirs with Christ, raised from the dead and given glorified bodies that are no longer subject to sin and death when Christ returns.

But all of this hinges on a real man named Jesus who was fully God, yet emptied himself of His divine privileges and became fully man in order to identify with us in our weakness and frailty. Though He was tempted in every way that we are and suffered in every way we do, He did not sin. Unlike us, He was innocent, but He suffered a criminal's death on the cross, bearing the full weight of our sin against God. Jesus lived as the perfect image bearer, fully reflecting the character of our holy God. As such, He was a suitable sacrifice to pay for the sins of man. God affirmed this by raising Christ from the dead in a glorified body, one that will never again know death.

Because Jesus lived, died, and was resurrected in a human body, we too will be raised and given new bodies—real flesh and blood bodies. We will run, jump, play, dance, sing, work, serve, eat, live, and love as we never have before. And it will be a glorious display of the power of God:

> Our Creator, the Master Artist, will put us on display to a wide-eyed universe. Our revelation will be an unveiling, and we will be seen as what we are, as what we were intended to be—God's image bearers. We will glorify him by ruling over the physical universe with creativity and camaraderie, showing respect and benevolence for all we rule. We will be revealed at our resurrection, when our adoption will be finalized and our bodies redeemed. We will be fully human, with righteous spirits and incorruptible bodies.[7]

Because we will have real flesh and blood bodies when Christ ushers in the new heaven and new earth, we live with anticipation rather than discouragement or despair. We live knowing that there is so much more to come. And we can endure with joy and peace as we await the day when we are finally given our new bodies.

EMBODIED IMAGE BEARERS

We were created to reflect the image of God and to live as His representatives in this world, and our bodies are crucial to living out God's purposes.

> Our physical bodies are a very important part of our existence and, as transformed when Christ returns, they will continue to be part of our existence for all eternity. Our bodies therefore have been created by God as suitable instruments to represent in a physical way our human nature, which has been made to be like God's own nature. In fact, almost everything we do is done by means of the use of our physical bodies— our thinking, our moral judgments, our prayer and praise, our demonstrations of love and concern for each other—all are done using the physical bodies God has given us.[8]

Everything we do as an embodied image bearer reflects the nature of God. Do your exercise routines, wardrobe choices, diet regimens, self-deprecating humor, and obsession with appearance rightly reflect the nature of God and point others back to Him? Or do you strive to reflect and represent your own nature and point others to yourself? Do you love your body as one who has been entrusted with its care? Or do you neglect it or indulge it as if it is yours to do with as you please? And how do your thoughts, feelings, and actions toward your body misrepresent God and the good body He created and entrusted to you?

The hope-filled reality of your body is this: You were created in the image of God; therefore, your body has value. Your body may be broken and corrupted, but that does not render you valueless. Your body is a temple. God lives in you, and that gives you value beyond any other gift. And your body is immortal, which gives you value here and now, not just there and then. And none of this is performance driven. It is not based on your exercise regimen or the foods you eat or whether or not you fit the cultural ideal of beauty. It is solely based on the grace of God who created you in His image, sent Christ to redeem you from the corruption of sin and death, and will recreate you with a body that can no longer be corrupted.

With all of this in clear view, our response should be like that of David when he declares, "Thank you for making me so wonderfully complex! Your workmanship is marvelous—how well I know it" (Psalms 139:14 NLT). Is that your response to the God who created you? Do you think of yourself this way? Do you worship Him and thank Him for His marvelous workmanship?

Questions for Reflection

1. How does the promised future of your new body affect how you live here and now? How does it affect the hope and contentment you have here and now?

2. Jesus lived in a real, human body that grew weary, hungry, and suffered just like we do. What is the significance of Jesus' embodiment to you as an embodied woman? Discuss as a group.

3. You were created to bear and reflect God's image in and through your body. What might your thoughts and actions regarding your body communicate to others about God?

3

DISEASED VISION

Several years ago my husband and I were at the local YMCA getting a little exercise. As we walked around the track upstairs, we watched those who were downstairs below us. On one of our laps around the track, my husband made a remark about some of the men who were lifting weights. His comment merited a response that I couldn't give him because I had not really been watching the men. I would glance in their general direction, but I wasn't paying them much attention. I had been intently watching the women. I was keenly aware of what they were wearing, what they looked like, and how fit they were. I gazed on almost every detail, sizing them up and measuring myself against them.

There was one particular woman who was at the gym every time we went, and we had come to know her through our time at the gym together. She was always very kind and friendly, but I could barely engage her in conversation because I was so envious of how fit and beautiful she was. Whenever I was around her, I was riddled with insecurity. Though I didn't consciously think it, deep down I believed she was a threat to my worth and identity—so much so that I went into self-preservation mode and began to judge her so I could feel better about myself. Though I knew little to nothing about her character, I labeled her as superficial because she spent so much time at the gym.

I wish I could say that is the only time something like that has happened, but sadly it is not. While that particular example is extreme, my struggle with comparison is as common and natural as breathing. I walk into a room, scan my surroundings, and eventually set my gaze on someone or something. It could be a woman who has on a super cute outfit or a woman with a slender frame. It may be a woman who is physically stunning or one who is the life of the party. Whatever it is that catches my eye, I see it, notice my lack, and begin to crave what I don't have.

This cycle is indicative of an undercurrent of discontent that lies buried beneath the surface in the lives of many women. Contrary to what many believe, **bodily discontent and insecurity are not a byproduct of our culture or media. These things only expose what is within the heart of a woman, which is a restless desire to elevate herself in ways her Creator never intended**. And we can trace this all the way back to the very first woman.

God created a bountiful garden full of life and every good thing, and He placed Adam and Eve in the Garden and gave them freedom to enjoy the abundance that surrounded them. They were free to eat, to explore, and to enjoy all that God had created. There was only one thing God withheld from them—the fruit of the tree in the center of the Garden, which the Lord called "the tree of the knowledge of good and evil." They were "naked and unashamed" (Genesis 2:25). They were vulnerable, fully exposed to one another and to God physically, spiritually, and emotionally. There was no barrier between them— no insecurity, envy, or embarrassment. Nothing hindered them. And they were at peace with one another, with God, and with themselves.

But not all was good in the Garden. In Genesis 3, the shrewdest of all God's wild creatures sets out to destroy God's good creation. The serpent, identifying a point of weakness, launches his attack on Eve. He appeals to the lust in her heart, drawing her gaze on the fruit of the forbidden tree. God had given Eve everything she *needed* to flourish. But her eyes drifted to what she didn't have, and she lost sight of God's gracious provision. Setting her gaze upon the fruit, she was deceived and became convinced she needed it.

> The woman was convinced. She saw that the tree was beautiful and its fruit looked delicious, and she wanted the wisdom it would give her. So she took some of the fruit and ate it. Then she gave some to her husband, who was with her, and he ate it, too. At that moment their eyes were opened, and they suddenly felt shame at their nakedness. So they sewed fig leaves together to cover themselves. And they heard the sound of the Lord God walking in the garden in the cool of the day, and the man and his wife hid themselves from the presence of the Lord God among the trees of the garden.
>
> ~ Genesis 3:6–8 NLT

The serpent appealed to Eve's desire to have something she didn't—wisdom—and to be something she wasn't—God. The longer Eve gazed on the fruit, the more impaired her vision became, and eventually she began to crave what she thought it would give her. So she took some and she ate, and she gave some to her husband who was with her. In that moment their eyes were opened. They became aware of good and evil, sin and death. The peace Adam and Eve had with each other, with God, and within themselves was destroyed. Now aware of their own nakedness and ashamed before one another, they covered themselves, and they hid from God when they heard Him walking in the Garden.

Eve's story illustrates the cycle of sin. This same cycle repeats itself in our lives on a daily basis. James warns us that "Temptation comes from our own desires, which entice us and drag us away. These desires give birth to sinful actions. And when sin is allowed to grow, it gives birth to death" (James 1:14–15 NLT). Eve saw and she desired—she *coveted*. She focused her gaze, set her heart on what she saw, and acted upon her desire. And the result was death and destruction for all mankind.

Questions for Reflection

1. When you think about your body, what is it you desire? Why?

2. Have you acted on your desires? How?

3. How did Eve's choice to reach for what she desired communicate what she believed about God? Discuss as a group.

4. Do the things you see on television, in magazines, and on social media create desire in you? How do you respond do those desires?

DISEASED VISION

Eve had tunnel vision. As her awareness of the fruit grew in the foreground, the abundance that surrounded her faded into the background. *Eve's eyes led her body.* About halfway through Jesus' famous Sermon on the Mount, Jesus makes an interesting statement about the eyes:

> Your eye is a lamp that provides light for your body. When your eye is good, your whole body is filled with light. But when your eye is bad, your whole body is filled with darkness. And if the light you think you have is actually darkness, how deep that darkness is!
>
> ~ Matthew 6:22–23 NLT

Jesus says that the eye, the *ophthalmos* in the original language, is a lamp for the body. In Scripture the "eye" is often synonymous with the "heart." That is to say that "setting the heart" and "fixing the eye" on something are phrases that can be used interchangeably.[1] If the eye is *good*, if it is healthy and clear, then your whole body will be full of light. But if it is bad, if it is blind or diseased, then your whole body will be full of darkness. The idea in view here is that if the eye is good then it is sound, it is single-focused, which "prevents it from becoming needlessly distracted"[2] or like James said, enticed by our own desires.

Our vision affects everything we do. If our eyes are clear, if they are single-focused, then we are able to see, judge, act, and react correctly. But if our eyes are bad, that is if we suffer from things like blurred or double vision, nearsightedness, or farsightedness, then our ability to see, judge, act, and react becomes impaired. This is true in a physical sense, but according to Jesus, it is just as true in a spiritual sense. As theologian John Stott says:

> Just as our eye affects our whole body, so our ambition (where we fix our eyes and our heart), affects our whole life . . . It's all a question of vision. If we have physical vision, we can see what we are doing and where we are going. So too if we have spiritual vision, if our spiritual perspective is correctly adjusted, then our life is filled with purpose and drive. But if our vision becomes clouded by the false gods of materialism, and we lose our sense of values, then our whole life is in darkness and we cannot see where we are going.[3]

Eve's vision was impaired; she was enticed by her own desires, and they lured her away from all that God had for her in the Garden. She became a slave to her desire, and the result was destruction not just for her but for all of humanity as well. For us, Eve provides us with not just an example to avoid but also a barometer of our own hearts. Far too often we succumb to the same temptation, choosing what we think will satisfy and missing out on all God has for us. The Lord does not intend for us to be slaves *to* our bodies or *for* our bodies. Nor does He intend for us to be slaves to our sinful desires; this kind of slavery results in death and despair. We will always be slaves, whether to our own desires or to righteousness. But there is only one kind of slavery that leads to life.

> Don't you realize that you become the slave of whatever you choose to obey? You can be a slave to sin, which leads

to death, or you can choose to obey God, which leads to righteous living. Thank God! Once you were slaves of sin, but now you wholeheartedly obey this teaching we have given you. Now you are free from your slavery to sin, and you have become slaves to righteous living.

~ Romans 6:16–18 NLT

Just as impaired physical vision has symptoms, impaired spiritual vision has symptoms as well. If we want to avoid the slavery of our own evil desires and become slaves to righteousness, our vision, our hearts must change.

Questions for Reflection

1. Paul said you are a slave to whatever you obey. Who/what are you "obeying" regarding your body? Yourself? Culture? God?

2. What are the effects of that obedience on your life? Slavery to sin and death? Or slavery to righteousness and life?

3. How has your vision become obscured? Where have you set your gaze? How is it affecting your ability to see, judge, act, and react in a way that leads to life?

SYMPTOMS OF DISEASED VISION

Honestly, identifying and examining our vision can be helpful in freeing us from the enticing lure of our own sinful desires. What are several symptoms that may reveal we have diseased vision?

SYMPTOM #1: ENVY

Envy is rampant in this age of discontentment. Envy is covetousness, or desiring what someone else has. It is a "painful or resentful awareness of an advantage enjoyed by another, joined with a desire to possess the same advantage."[4] Eve desired the fruit because she wanted to be wise like God. Similarly, a woman envies another woman because she wants what the other woman has over what God has entrusted to her. The inner dialog of envy often sounds like, "She's so petite; I wish I looked like that." Or, "She looks like she's lost weight. I wish I had the kind of willpower." Or, "She always looks so cute and stylish and confident. I guess if I had money like she does, I could look like that too."

This symptom of diseased vision is insidious and divisive to the body of Christ. It produces bitterness and resentment over the "perceived advantages" of another. If it is allowed to fester, it not only threatens our relationship with others, it also threatens our relationship with God. It is why one woman may choose friends whom she views as less attractive than she, or why another woman gets frustrated with God for the way He made her.

In Matthew 20:1–15, Jesus tells a story about the kingdom of heaven being like a landowner who went out early in the morning to hire laborers for his vineyard. He went out at nine o'clock in the morning, hired some laborers, and agreed to pay them a fair wage. He went out again at noon and at three o'clock and hired more laborers, promising them a fair wage as well. Then at five o'clock in the afternoon, he went out again and saw some laborers standing around.

When he asked them why they weren't working, they responded that no one had hired them. So he sent them out into his field also.

An hour later, at six o'clock, the landowner told the foreman to call all the laborers in from the field and pay each of them, beginning with those hired last, for one day's labor. When those who were hired at nine o'clock in the morning saw that the landowner paid those hired at five o'clock in the afternoon a full day's wage, they assumed they would be paid more. But when they received the same wage as those who had only worked one hour, they began to grumble among themselves. So the landowner responded to them,

> "I am not being unfair to you, friend. Didn't you agree to work for a denarius? Take your pay and go. I want to give the one who was hired last the same as I gave you. Don't I have the right to do what I want with my own money? Or are you envious because I am generous?"
>
> ~ vv. 13–15 NIV

The question is piercing. "Are you envious because I am generous?" Interestingly, the word Jesus uses for envy in this passage is *ophthalmos*, which is the same word he uses for "eye" when he said, "the eye is the lamp of the body" (Matthew 6:22–23).[5] By doing this, Jesus connects the eye to envy. A more literal translation of the landowner's question is: "Is your eye evil because mine is good?" Within this specific parable, the laborers, **seeing** the generosity of the landowner toward those hired late in the day **gave rise to envy** within them. Rather than being grateful for the landowner's generosity *toward them*, they were frustrated about his generosity *toward others* who didn't have to work as long or hard as they did (vv. 11–12). But it is the landowner's money, his land, and his right to determine how to distribute it among the workers. Likewise, God owns all, and it is His right to be generous with it however and to whomever He wishes.

When I think about the laborers grumbling against the landowner, I can't help but be reminded of my own grumbling against God. Many times I've wanted to accuse Him of being unfair in the distribution of gifts—everything ranging from marriage to metabolism. Envy impairs your ability to see the good gifts God has entrusted to you. If your eye is good, then you will see clearly, and it will bring light and direction to your life. But if your eye is bad, *if it is obstructed by envy*, then your whole life will be dark.

Envy is poisonous to our spiritual condition. Proverbs 14:30 says, "A heart at peace gives life to the body, but envy rots the bones" (NIV). Envy rots you from the inside out. It robs you of the ability to enjoy the good gifts God has given you. When envy is allowed to remain, you are not free to love others or fully engage them, because your hearts and minds are occupied with the things of self. But a heart at peace brings life to your body—mentally, physically, emotionally, and spiritually (Proverbs 14:30). This kind of peace is indicative of wholeness. It is a deep, abiding peace that cannot be found in external reality or in circumstances. You may be at peace with your thirty-year-old body, but you will one day have a sixty-year-old body. Or you may be at peace with your body that is currently able to function like an athlete, but it will one day function like a grandmother. You may even be at peace with the way your hair looks today, but tomorrow is a new day. Our emotions are fickle, and circumstances are ever changing. The kind of peace that brings life to the body can be found only in something that never changes—that one is God.

The prophet Isaiah said, "You will keep in perfect peace all who trust in you, all whose thoughts are fixed on you" (Isaiah 26:3 NLT). Fixing your thoughts on the Lord means reminding yourself often of His character, of His goodness and faithfulness *to you*. It is to remind yourself that He withholds no good thing from you but gives you everything you *need* for living a godly life (1 Peter 1:3 NLT). It is to rest on His great and precious promises that enable you to share in His divine nature and escape the world's corruption, which is caused by our human desires (1 Peter 1:4 NLT). God alone is steady and true. He alone is a safe place to rest our trust, to find our security and value.

When a woman experiences this kind of peace, she is able to be at rest with who God created her to be, the distinct way in which she is embodied, and with what God has entrusted to her (as well as what He hasn't). She is not driven by her desire to possess what another has or by self-pity over what she perceives she lacks, because she knows God has been gracious and merciful to her. And so she is free to receive God's good gifts and to offer them back in service to Him and others.

SYMPTOM #2: COMPARISON AND JUDGMENT

Comparison and judgment is another symptom of diseased vision. Judgment is "the process of forming an opinion or evaluation by discerning and comparing."[6] *Judgment is forming an opinion through comparison.* Judgment and comparison are bedfellows. The judgment, comparison, and competition present among so many women is detrimental to our spiritual maturity and to our relationships with one another. Insecurity and feelings of inadequacy are often at the root of comparison and judgment.

When placed in a group of men and women, whether at a party or at the beach or even at a PTA meeting, most women will spend more time looking at one another than they will looking at the men in the room. As a woman surveys the landscape in front of her, she scans each woman in the room, evaluates her, and then discerns where she lands by comparison. This is common among women of every age and season of life. A woman who is not self-conscious about her body or her appearance may instead struggle with comparing her husband to another woman's husband, her children to someone else's children, her career to another woman's career, or even her home to another woman's home.

There are two dangers to a woman's soul when she does this. She will either become proud, believing herself to be better, look better, have better than the other women around her. Or it will lead to shame, self-pity, or despair when she believes that she is not good enough or that she doesn't measure up. The problem with this is that **she is judging her insides, her value and worth, by another person's outsides, by the image they project**. She places her value, her security on a scale that goes up or down based on those she is measured against. But these scales aren't accurate; her vision is impaired. She has set her gaze on the wrong things.

The Apostle Paul understood this type of judgment—judgment based on an inaccurate understanding of what is truly valuable. In his letter to the church at Corinth, Paul addresses division that has sprung up among its members. Some of its members were choosing their favorite teachers, aligning themselves with them, and identifying themselves as followers of those men. Some chose Apollos, some Peter, some Paul, and the "super spiritual" among them chose Christ (1 Corinthians 1:10–12). Paul knows how divisive this is to the body of the church and confronts it head on. He does not spend time defending himself or trying to prove himself worthy of them. He does not attempt to bolster his own self-esteem, nor does he look to others to affirm him. Instead, Paul says,

> As for me, it matters very little how I might be evaluated by you or by any human authority. I don't even trust my own judgment on this point. My conscience is clear, but that doesn't prove I'm right. It is the Lord himself who will examine me and decide.
>
> ~ 1 Corinthians 4:3–4 NLT

Paul doesn't trust the judgment of others. He doesn't even trust his own judgment. This passage gives us insight into the kind of freedom Paul has, freedom that does not come through self-esteem. The reason we have a hard time finding anything like real freedom is because we have misdiagnosed the problem. We think the problem is that we need to feel better about ourselves, so we go about trying to fix all the things we think are wrong with us. **We attempt to treat an internal problem with an external solution**. But Paul is not deceived by envy or a desire to measure up. He is unconcerned with what others think of him or how they judge him. But this is not because his heart has been wounded and is calloused and self-protective. And it's not that Paul doesn't care. On the contrary, he does care; he just cares about the *right things*. Paul's vision was un-obstructed and clear; he was not trying to please both God and men (Galatians 1:10).

Paul carries this one step further. Not only is he unconcerned with how others evaluate or judge him, he doesn't even judge him-self. He doesn't spend hours on end navel-gazing. Unlike Paul, many women have become consumed with how they feel about themselves. Feelings of inadequacy and insecurity drive many women to spend inordinate amounts of time and money on cosmetic surgery, gym memberships, and weight-loss programs—anything that might help them find peace within. But Paul knows better. He doesn't even trust his own judgment. Instead, he entrusts himself to the Lord as his judge. This is where he rests his hope, his value, and his worth.

Paul does care, but his vision is laser-focused—he is more con-cerned with God's judgment of him. And he knows that God's judg-ment has already been met, fully and finally, through Jesus Christ who absorbed God's judgment in our place. Because Paul finds his security in what Jesus accomplished for him on the cross, he is not driven by insecurities, desires for acceptance and approval, or fear of rejection. He is free to not be everyone's favorite. He is free to not be admired. And because he is not driven by his own sinful desires, he is free to obey God and love and serve others faithfully. Paul's gaze is set solely on the Lord, knowing that there and only there can he truly be secure. We cannot please both God and men. We cannot even please God and ourselves. Our hearts are divided; our flesh and spirit war against one another.

The good news of the gospel is that Jesus forfeited His security with the Father so that He could take on your insecurity at the cross. In Christ, you are holy, blameless, accepted, pleasing, and loved. Your identity is eternally secure. You no longer have to fear what others think of you or be driven by what you think of yourself. When you embrace this like Paul, you are freed from the tyranny of self and are able to engage and love one another without comparing and competing. You are freed to steward your body in a way that honors God in gratitude and serves others in love, not because you are trying to earn their favor.

SYMPTOM #3: DISCONTENTMENT & ENTITLEMENT

A woman in a state of discontent is not pleased or satisfied with what she has and often feels a sense of grievance and a restless aspiration for improvement.[7] This discontentment is often coupled with a sense of entitlement or a belief that you deserve better.[8] This is yet another symptom of impaired vision.

Discontentment may be present in a woman who is frustrated with her large calves or thick ankles, or it may be in a woman who is preoccupied with her crooked nose or large ears. As she gazes on those who have what she perceives to be the ideal, her discontentment grows, and a sense of entitlement rises up within her. She begins to believe she deserves to have freckle-free skin or long lean legs. Discontentment and entitlement may also be present in a woman who feels frustrated over her aging body that can no longer pick up her grandchildren, or in a woman whose infertility has left her unable to bear children, or in a woman who struggles with a disease that riddles her with chronic pain. While some of these frustrations, especially the ones involving physical infirmities, are valid issues, it is important to be mindful of your responses to them. How you see, judge, act, and react to your circumstances, whether your physical appearance or your body's ability to function, will determine the measure of peace you have with yourself, with God, and with others.

If you find that you are irritable, restless, and discontent with your current situation or circumstances, you may be tempted to become frustrated with the Lord. You may also be tempted to make demands of Him, expecting Him to satisfy the unfulfilled longings of your heart. It is like the clay pot that argues with his maker, to which the Lord replies,

> What sorrow awaits those who argue with their Creator. Does a clay pot argue with its maker? Does the clay dispute with the one who shapes it, saying, "Stop, you're doing it wrong!" Does the pot exclaim, "How clumsy can you be?"

> How terrible it would be if a newborn baby said to its father, "Why was I born?" or if it said to its mother, "Why did you make me this way?"

> This is what the Lord says—the Holy One of Israel and your Creator: "Do you question what I do for my children? Do you give me orders about the work of my hands?

"I am the one who made the earth and created people to live on it. With my hands I stretched out the heavens. All the stars are at my command."

~ Isaiah 45:9–12 NLT

A clay pot arguing with its maker about how to be made sounds ridiculous, but it is the same thing we do when we complain about our own bodies. Discontentment with how God made you or the circumstances that have befallen you discounts the goodness of God who is not only aware of your circumstances but is also at work in the midst of them. When you choose to be discontent, you place yourself above God as His judge, believing you know better what is fair, right, or just. But this only increases frustration and will never lead to the contentment and peace you desire. Instead of a feeling of fullness and joy within, it brings emptiness and despair. Rather than promoting unity and fellowship with God and others, it brings division, resentment, and feelings of entitlement.

While it is important to resist the temptations toward discontent and feelings of entitlement, it is also important not to minimize our struggles with the body and to acknowledge that there is legitimate grief that accompanies being embodied. Our bodies still suffer the effects of living in a fallen world. They don't always function as they are supposed to function. Some are marked by deformities, and others are scarred from injuries. Some battle chronic illnesses that imprison them in their own bodies. This is not the way it is supposed to be. Grief is an appropriate response to the brokenness we experience. However, we need to be mindful that we do not allow legitimate grief to turn into self-pity and despair. It is important that we are intentional in shepherding our own souls through this process. In our moments of grief, we must preach the truth of God's promised restoration. Though our bodies aren't what they should be right now, one day God will make everything new, including our bodies. No longer will they be subject to deformities, chronic illness, or death. This is the hope we have that fuels contentment in the midst of legitimate grief.

Discontentment not only affects you personally, it also robs you of the power to serve the body of Christ in the way you were distinctly created to serve. Paul addresses this very thing in his letter to the Corinthians who were divided over the appropriation of spiritual gifts. They were elevating the more public gifts, gifts that were seen as more spiritual—speaking in tongues or teaching—over gifts of service and hospitality. This bred envy, division, and discontent in the church as those who lacked the more public gifts felt marginalized and devalued. But Paul encourages and exhorts them, reminding them that each believer is a part of the whole body of Christ and is entrusted with gifts necessary to building up the church.

> But our bodies have many parts, and God has put each part just where he wants it. How strange a body would be if it had only one part! Yes, there are many parts, but only one body. The eye can never say to the hand, "I don't need you." The head can't say to the feet, "I don't need you."

> In fact, some parts of the body that seem weakest and least important are actually the most necessary. And the parts we

regard as less honorable are those we clothe with the greatest care. So we carefully protect those parts that should not be seen, while the more honorable parts do not require this special care. So God has put the body together such that extra honor and care are given to those parts that have less dignity. This makes for harmony among the members, so that all the members care for each other. If one part suffers, all the parts suffer with it, and if one part is honored, all the parts are glad.

~ 1 Corinthians 12:18–26 NLT

Paul knows and believes that God has created each person distinctly to meet a need of the larger church body. If we despise the way we were created and abdicate our responsibility to use the gifts entrusted to us, the whole body suffers; we are not free to love others well. Likewise, if we are conceited and use our gifts to make us feel better about ourselves, the whole body suffers; we are still not free to love others well. To be on either extreme is to be consumed with self and not free to love and serve those in the body of Christ.

But this does not just apply to the appropriation of spiritual gifts; it also applies to the physical body. If a woman is preoccupied with self-pity or despair over her weight, the shape of her body, or the physical challenges entrusted to her, then she is not free to love and serve those around her. Because her vision is turned inward, she is unable to see the needs of those around her. Similarly, if a woman has become her own self-improvement project, shaping and trimming and defining her body into something she can be proud of, then she is still not free to love and serve her neighbors. She is too wrapped up in herself to identify and meet the needs of others. A woman is just as prideful and narcissistic in conceit as she is in despair because the focus is always on the self.

Questions for Reflection

1. When you see physical beauty (or spiritual beauty) that exceeds your own in other women, which of these words best describe your initial reaction: envy, judgment, discontentment, or entitlement?

2. How is your vision obstructed by envy? By judgment? By discontentment? How does this impact your ability to see, think, act, and react in faith and obedience?

3. Think about the relationships you have with other women around whom you are the most free and comfortable. How do these women compare to you physically? What might this reveal about you?

4. In what ways are you discontent with your physical appearance? Are you more discontent with your physical appearance or your pursuit of holiness? Why?

5. How do you respond to feelings of envy, discontentment, or entitlement? Do they drive you toward the pursuit of perfection or toward apathy and despair?

6. What kind of compliments do you give most often? Are they mostly based on appearance? What might this indicate about what you value?

THE ROLE OF LOVE

God intentionally and distinctly created each woman and entrusted her with certain gifts and abilities. This is for the good of

God's church, the bride of Christ. We belong to God and to one another. We exist to bring glory to God and to build up His church. And we can't do this when we are preoccupied with ourselves and consumed with pride or insecurity. In his letter to the Corinthians, Paul exhorts believers to stop focusing on one-upping one another and instead own who God has created them to be. This exhortation is for us as well. It will help us refocus our gaze and show us a way of life that is best of all (1 Corinthians 12:31b).

> If I could speak all the languages of earth and of angels, but didn't love others, I would only be a noisy gong or a clanging cymbal. If I had the gift of prophecy, and if I understood all of God's secret plans and possessed all knowledge, and if I had such faith that I could move mountains, but didn't love others, I would be nothing. If I gave everything I have to the poor and even sacrificed my body, I could boast about it; but if I didn't love others, I would have gained nothing.
>
> ~ 1 Corinthians 13:1–3 NLT

We could reframe Paul's exhortation around body matters and the truth would still resound loud and clear:

> If I were petite and looked great in a bikini, but I did not love others, I would only be an object to look at and admire. If I had the gift of self-discipline, and if I had great knowledge about nutritional health, and if I exercised my body every day and made it my slave, but I didn't love others, I would be nothing. If I rejected physical appearance and fo-

cused only on spiritual matters, I could boast about it; but if I didn't love others, I would have gained nothing.

Paul's message is strong and piercing. Love for God and for one another is the highest call; it is the thing believers should aspire to above and beyond anything else in this world. Paul continues by diagnosing love:

> Love is patient and kind. Love is not jealous or boastful or proud or rude. It does not demand its own way. It is not irritable, and it keeps no record of being wronged. It does not rejoice about injustice but rejoices whenever the truth wins out. Love never gives up, never loses faith, is always hopeful, and endures through every circumstance.
>
> ~ 1 Corinthians 13:4–7 NLT

Paul knows that preoccupation with self is harmful to the whole body of Christ, and it is also harmful to us. Does Paul's description of love describe you where body matters are concerned? A woman who is governed by love does not envy the beauty, body, or abilities of others. She does not boast over her own accomplishments. She is not proud of how fit she is, nor is she proud of how self-controlled she is where food is concerned. She is not jealous of others, nor does she rejoice when she perceives others to be less attractive. She does not demand her own way or feel entitled to more than what God has entrusted to her. Regardless of her challenges or disappointments, a woman governed by love never gives up, never loses faith, is always hopeful, and endures through every circumstance. She knows and

believes that God created her body, redeemed her body, and will recreate her body when Christ returns, so she is free to steward it self-
lessly, offer it sacrificially, and spend it lavishly in love and service to
God and others.

The question before us is this: Is love for God and others governing how we see, judge, act, and react toward our bodies? Likewise, is
love for God and others governing how we see, judge, act, and react
toward others? Does this kind of love for God and others define you?
Are you genuinely able to celebrate the good gifts of another without feeling in some way that you don't measure up? Are you able to
genuinely love those you feel are prettier, skinnier, healthier, or more
successful than you? What about those you think aren't?

The problem for the Corinthians and for many of us is diseased
vision. We are focused on and enamored with the wrong things,
things that will pass away—chasing after the wind and never catch-
ing it (Ecclesiastes 1:14). We are looking for satisfaction in things that
will never bring contentment. Love is others focused, but when it
comes to our bodies, many women are busy gazing in the mirror. No
matter how good we are, no matter how fit or healthy, no matter how
fashionable or put together, no matter how good we look in a bath-
ing suit, no matter what others think of us or even what we think of
ourselves—all of these things are temporary; they are fleeting. Only
three things will last forever: faith, hope, and love. And love, Paul
says, is the greatest of them all (1 Corinthians 13:13 NLT).

I wonder what it would look like if a whole generation of women began to love people more than we need them. If rather than looking to others for acceptance and approval, we humbly received the acceptance and approval God longs to extend to us. What would happen if we stopped commiserating with one another over perceived flaws and stopped co-laboring alongside one another in the pursuit of perfection, and instead challenged one another to grow in godliness and co-labored alongside one another in service to the body of Christ? What would happen if we helped one another find freedom from the tyranny of self, in the form of pride or insecurity, and helped each other become powerful women of God who are known by their love for God and one another?

Jesus, nearing the time of His arrest and crucifixion, stole away from the crowds to spend precious time with His disciples. As they prepared to share the Passover meal with one another, Jesus did the unthinkable. He took off His robe, wrapped a towel around His waist, and began washing His disciples' feet. After he finished, he said to them,

> "Do you understand what I was doing? You call me 'Teacher' and 'Lord,' and you are right, because that's what I am. And since I, your Lord and Teacher, have washed your feet, you ought to wash each other's feet. I have given you an example to follow. Do as I have done to you. I tell you the truth, slaves are not greater than their master. Nor is the messenger more important than the one who sends the message. Now that you know these things, God will bless you for doing them"

> ~ John 13:12b–17 NLT

It is hard to envy, compare, or judge another when your focus is on loving and serving them. In His final hours of His earthly ministry, Jesus used His body in service to His disciples. He spent three years with these men, teaching them, feeding them, challenging them, rebuking them, serving them, protecting them, and loving them. Jesus, the Lord and King of the universe, did not self-protect or self-promote. He did not aspire to earthly greatness and glory, but instead He stooped to serve in love. And as He told them, He also tells us, people will know we are His disciples when we love one another (John 13:34–35).

Questions for Reflection

1. Have you ever missed part of a conversation because you were wondering what someone else was thinking about you or your appearance?

2. Have you ever postponed or canceled a date, appointment, errand, or meeting because you were not happy with your appearance? If so, were you honest about why you canceled, or did you make an excuse?

3. Jesus said that we should love our neighbor as we love ourselves (Matthew 22:29). What might it look like for you to love another "as yourself"?

4

EXPOSING OUR IDOLS

MISDIAGNOSED

When I was a little girl, my dad endured a major health crisis. Over the course of one year, his health rapidly declined. Though he was eating six or seven times a day, he lost thirty pounds. Most of his clothes were ruined due to extreme heat sensitivity and profuse sweating. His *resting* heart rate was around 125 beats per minute, as though he had just completed a marathon. The effects of his illness began taking its toll on his work and his relationships. He described each day as slogging through knee-deep mud. Nothing was easy. His productivity and effectiveness at work decreased by around thirty percent. And the onslaught of anxiety and depression strained his marriage and his ability to be available mentally, emotionally, or physically for his family.

After one year and many doctors' visits later, he was still no closer to a solution, and his condition grew worse. He knew there was something physical going on with him, but his doctor insisted that it was only anxiety and depression, never looking past the surface issue for a deeper root cause. Though the doctor attempted to treat his symptoms, his condition continued to deteriorate. Then one day he visited an internist who diagnosed him with Graves' disease. They had finally discovered the root cause beneath all the symptoms, and as a result, he began to get better.

My dad was suffering from a debilitating illness, which was robbing him of the life and vitality a thirty-two year old man should have. There was something invisible going on with him, something that lay hidden beneath the surface. Treating the surface issues didn't bring him relief and freedom from the disease that had him in its grips. In fact, it only prolonged the problem. It was only when someone looked beneath the surface and identified the root problem that real healing began.

As women seeking to make peace with our bodies, it is possible that we have neglected to look beneath the symptoms and, as a result, have misdiagnosed the problem. It is possible that we have been attempting to treat an internal, spiritual problem with external, physical solutions such as diets, anti-aging products, plastic surgery, cosmetics, fashion, and exercise. When that fails to produce desirable results, we may swing to the other extreme, practicing self-affirmation and striving to increase self-esteem. But as our condition continues to deteriorate, we resign ourselves to an "it is what it is" mentality.

This is not to say that there aren't very real physical challenges that shape our embodied existence. On the contrary, because our bodies are broken, we still suffer pain, disability, disease, and even deformities.

All of these may, at times, require physical treatment. It is also not to negate that there are deep emotions tethered to the challenges of our embodiment, whether in its form (appearance) or its functionality (how it works or doesn't work). But far too many books have been written either addressing the emotions—focusing on boosting self-acceptance and self-esteem, or addressing the body itself—focusing on sculpting, shaping, and dieting as a way to happiness.

THE DIAGNOSIS – DISORDERED WORSHIP

Just like my dad's disease, the issue many women have with their bodies may be the symptom of a deeper problem. This is not just an issue of **self-acceptance**: loving yourself as you are. Nor is it just an issue of **self-management**: focusing on things like diet and exercise as a means to contentment. Both of those approaches fail to go much beyond the surface issue. And the irony of many of these prescriptions for happiness and contentment is that they begin and end with the self. If we are courageous enough to peer beneath the surface, we may discover that self-centeredness is the root of many of our issues. And to treat the self with the self is just as ludicrous as treating a hangover with alcohol.

For many women, bodily dissatisfaction (or even bodily pride) is actually just a symptom of being overly concerned with one's self. It is evidenced in the constant assessing of one's appearance, desires, feelings, and abilities. The word we use for this kind of self-absorption is *narcissism*. Narcissus was a well-known character from Greek mythology who fell in love with himself upon seeing his reflection in a pool of water.[1] He became so enamored with his own image that he was unable to pull himself away from the pool, and as a result, he died. Narcissus was fixated on himself; he was self-absorbed. Many women may initially have trouble identifying with Narcissus because rather than falling in love with their own reflection, they loathe it. **But whether we loathe ourselves or love ourselves, self is still at the center.**

If our gaze is constantly drifting to the reflection staring back at us, it may be that we have been lured to the pool like Narcissus and have become enamored with our own image. And whether we find it alluring or repulsive, we just cannot stop looking. Like a baby just discovering her feet or her tongue, we are absorbed, mesmerized. This is a debilitating human condition. Its effects are far-reaching, stretching beyond a woman's view of herself to how she sees and interacts with the world around her. Fear of man and desire to be accepted imprisons a woman to her own self-image. This is the disease of self-centeredness—placing oneself at the center. Ultimately, this is an issue of **disordered worship: worshiping and serving oneself instead of God.**

We were created to worship. In fact, one of the very first commands given the Israelites was to love the Lord with all their heart, soul, and strength (Deuteronomy 6:5), a command that Jesus affirmed during his ministry (Mark 12:28–31). Because we were created to worship, we will either worship God, or we will worship something else. To worship something is to be devoted to it, to treasure it, and ascribe it ultimate worth and value. But Scripture is very clear that we are to worship God alone. Worshiping anything other than God is idolatry

(Exodus 20:3–6, 34:11–17). **Idolatry is to take a good thing and make it into an ultimate thing, elevating it to god-like status.**

We get a first glimpse of idolatry in Exodus 32. The Lord had delivered the people of Israel out of their slavery in Egypt through great displays of power and miracles. His personal presence was with them, leading them through the wilderness in a cloud by day and fire by night (Exodus 13:21–22). He conquered their enemies by swallowing them up in the Red Sea (Exodus 14). He provided the Israelites with water and food in the desert (Exodus 16 & 17). But not long into their miraculous deliverance, while God was meeting with Moses on Mt. Sinai, the people grew fearful and restless. God's tangible presence was not with them, and they longed to attach their hope, security, and worship to something. So they crafted an image of a calf, and they fell down and worshiped it (Exodus 32), *rejoicing in the work of their own hands* (Acts 7:41).

The Israelites craved assurance of God's presence with them and when they didn't have it, rather than exercising faith, they took matters into their own hands. Rather than being devoted to God and entrusting themselves to him alone, they were devoted to their own desires for comfort, power, control, and assurance. This is not unlike the idolatry of our day and time. But rather than the carefully constructed image of a golden calf, it is the carefully constructed image of a woman. This is the very essence of idolatry.

In his book *Counterfeit Gods*, Tim Keller defines idolatry as:

> Anything more important to you than God, anything
> that absorbs your heart and imagination more than God,

anything you seek to give you what only God can give. [It] is anything so central and essential to your life that, should you lose it, your life would feel hardly worth living. _An idol has such a controlling position in your heart that you can spend most of your passion and energy, your emotional and financial resources, on it without a second thought..._

An idol is whatever you look at and say, in your heart of hearts, "If I have that, then I'll feel my life has meaning, then I'll know I have value, then I'll feel significant and secure." There are many ways to describe that kind of relationship to something, but perhaps the best one is worship.[2]

If you think along those lines and how it relates to your body, what do you find yourself thinking or daydreaming about? With what are you most preoccupied? For some women it may be the idea that if they lose five more pounds they will feel secure. For others it may be saving up for a cosmetic procedure that promises to be the solution to lifelong insecurities. Or it may be the idea that having the right kind of clothes or hairstyle will help her fit in with her peers. How are you using certain things to bring you comfort or approval? How might you be using your body to try and attain power over something or control over someone? This may not be an easy question to answer, but it is important nonetheless. Whatever the "it" is that you find yourself spending most of your passion, energy, and emotional and financial resources on, has in some sense of the word become what you worship.

This disordered worship presents itself in many ways. For some women, disordered worship is evidenced in their relationship with food, though it may manifest itself differently according to each woman's individuality. For one woman, food represents comfort. She uses it to self-soothe and self-medicate during times of stress or discomfort. It may also be what she reaches for as a reward for working out extra hard, or her new promotion, or reaching a new milestone. Perhaps it is even her companion when she is bored or lonely. Food is an easy go-to, especially for women in our western culture. Though she would never think of food as being god-like for her, she continues to reach for it for comfort, pleasure, and even security, things only God can provide.

For another woman, food is more an issue of control. When everything else in her life feels out of control, food is something she has power over. She can eat or she can refuse to eat, whichever best suits her at the time. She may carefully weigh every portion and count every calorie. Food for her is not necessarily something to be enjoyed but is only fuel for her body. She may be so preoccupied with pesticides and processed foods that she drives to three or four stores and spends inordinate amounts of time and money to ensure her foods are safe for consumption. Her dietary choices are rigid, and she doesn't understand why other people insist on feeding her children junk food. She is frustrated when others don't provide "healthy" options and feels justified in her frustration. This is especially common in an age of "food-righteousness," where many are more vigilant about what they eat than they are about reading their Bibles and serving those less fortunate.

A woman who loves comfort may struggle with the discipline of exercising her body regularly. Rather than expending effort and energy through walking, running, hiking, swimming, or serving others, she prefers to go to a movie or watch television. Deep down she may feel like she should be more active, but she spiritualizes her lack of physical activity by telling herself that it's what is on the inside that counts. She might even find herself standing in judgment of all those girls who seem to focus so much time and energy on their outward appearance. To her, the body is going to die anyway, so she might as well enjoy life while she can. She has abandoned responsibility and instead of being a good steward of her body and finding comfort in Christ, she seeks ultimate comfort and pleasure here and now.

But for another woman, exercise may be a completely different matter. Strenuous physical activity makes her feel strong and powerful. She enjoys looking good in her clothes and likes the looks she receives from men and from other women. She works hard to maintain her body, and she is proud of the way it looks. She goes to great efforts to tone every troublesome part and reach new fitness goals. For her, exercise is a discipline in self-control, and she can't believe how many overweight and out of shape people there are in the world. She sometimes looks in disgust on those who have "let themselves go" and who don't go to the same effort she does to take care of themselves. Sometimes she even places her man-made traditions and attempts at righteousness on others, getting frustrated with her own friends and family when they don't follow her lead. She is unwilling to lose control of how others perceive her body. Because she cannot give up control in this area, she is not free to worship God; she is instead worshiping something else.

Many women, driven by a desire for approval, are slaves to the latest fashion trends. A woman who longs for the approval, even adoration, of others, struggles to leave the house without her hair and makeup done. She would not want to be caught dead looking less than her best at all times. She is always well put together and the envy of her friends. The attention she gets when she wears a new outfit or gets a fashionable new haircut fuels her even more. She is very intentional about what she wears, carefully weighing the events of the day and who she might see. Her beliefs about personal appearance extend to others as well, believing that all women should take good care of themselves and always look their best.

But then other women, whether driven by a desire for comfort or by fear that they will never measure up, settle into a rhythm of ball caps and lounge wear. A woman driven by her insecurity may hide the extra weight she's gained over the years behind baggy or blousy clothing. Perhaps the idea that a woman would spend time and energy on physical appearance seems less than spiritual to her, and so she comforts herself with her own self-righteousness. Or maybe despair has settled so deep in her bones that she has given up and rejects any efforts at self-care.

For the most part, food, exercise, and clothing are morally neutral issues; that is to say that, in and of themselves, they are not sinful. In fact, they are very good things given to us by God for our nourishment and enjoyment. Enjoying finding new recipes to cook, admiring how another woman dresses, or being diligent in self-care is not always indicative of idolatry. It is *when we allow these good things to become ultimate things*, when we are driven along by our passions for comfort, control, power, and approval that we corrupt these good God-given gifts. We begin to worship that which was created rather than worshiping the Creator; we begin to serve that which was created to serve us. For these women, what was a good thing becomes corrupted and entraps them, demanding their worship.

Our emotions are often helpful in identifying idolatry in our lives. If missing a workout ruins your day, this may be an indicator that your heart is searching for peace in something other than God. If eating an extra piece of chocolate cake makes you frustrated with yourself and others, of if the number on the scale determines your mood for the day, then perhaps an idol has taken root in your heart. But we should not be surprised when we find ourselves in the grips of idolatry. Many passages warn that to worship anything other than God will become a snare and lead to destruction (Exodus 23:33, Deuteronomy 7:25, Psalms 106:36, 1 Timothy 6:9).

There is perhaps no more compelling passage in Scripture on the foolishness of idolatry than one found in the book of Isaiah:

This is what the Lord says—Israel's King and Redeemer, the Lord of Heaven's Armies:

"I am the First and the Last; there is no other God.

Who is like me? Let him step forward and prove to you his power. Let him do as I have done since ancient times when I established a people and explained its future.

Do not tremble; do not be afraid. Did I not proclaim my purposes for you long ago? You are my witnesses—is there any other God? No! There is no other Rock—not one!"

How foolish are those who manufacture idols. These prized objects are really worthless. The people who worship idols don't know this, so they are all put to shame.

Who but a fool would make his own god—an idol that cannot help him one bit.

~ Isaiah 44:6–10 NLT

Isaiah uses strong language in this passage, contrasting the power of the one and only God who created the heavens and earth with the powerlessness of the idol: the power of the Creator versus the created. He mocks those who worship idols, "Who but a fool makes his own god?" While it seems harsh, the truth is plain to see. The foolishness of idolatry is that we would place our hope and security in something with no power to save us, something that is within our control.

The poor, deluded fool feeds on ashes. He trusts something that can't help him at all. Yet he cannot bring himself to ask, "Is this idol that I'm holding in my hand a lie?"

~ Isaiah 44:20 NLT

That message, though delivered thousands of years ago, is just as relevant today. In fact, we find a modern equivalent delivered by an actress named Lupita Nyongo during an acceptance speech. As a little girl, Lupita hated her dark skin. She looked around and didn't see other little girls like her. She pleaded and bargained with God, hoping He would make her skin lighter, only to wake up each morning and find the same dark-skinned little girl staring back at her in the mirror as the day before. To Lupita, her complexion was an "obstacle to overcome," and it consumed her thoughts. But Lupita's mother recognized that her daughter was enslaved to a lie, and she encouraged her with words that echo Isaiah's, "You can't eat beauty; it won't feed you."[3] Her mother recognized that beauty could never nourish or sustain her daughter. **To feed on beauty is to feed on ashes. It can't sustain us, nor was it ever intended to do so.** It can't free us from insecurity or feelings of inadequacy. Even if we have it or attain it, it is fleeting. Physical beauty is always subject to time, because given enough time, it will always give way to age, decay, and eventually to death.

This is important because so many women seek life in their physical appearance or their physical abilities. Like the fool in Isaiah's passage, they've placed their hope in an idol that cannot feed them or help them at all. And yet, they cannot seem to tell themselves that they are holding onto a lie (Isaiah 44:20). It is often easier to bury our head in the sand and rationalize our behavior, because entrusting ourselves to God is risky. It requires faith and dependence. But then that is the exact reason we turn to idols—we want something that we can control. And so we settle for the imprisonment of our illusion rather than the truth that can set us free.

Questions for Reflection

1. In what ways has your life become "centered" around your appearance?

2. If our emotions can be good indicators of what we value, what do your emotions say about what is most important to you? (For example: getting frustrated when your hair won't cooperate or crying when the scale is unkind)

3. How often do you tend to be allured or repulsed by your image? What is the problem with either one?

IDENTIFYING OUR IDOLS

If we hope to find anything like real freedom in this area, we need to discover the idols that are ruling our lives. Though there are likely many idols present in our lives, there are four that seem to be primary motivating factors or ambitions behind our behavior: comfort/pleasure, approval, control, and power.[4] Our quest for these often leads us further from the freedom God intends for His children. Though we may find all of these present in our lives in varying degrees, there may be one or two with which we identify most, especially where our bodies are concerned.

COMFORT/PLEASURE

When comfort is our motivation, we attempt to avoid unpleasant feelings, whether physical, mental, or emotional. A woman who has the idol of comfort may choose the easy way, the path of least resistance—where minimum work or effort is required. It may be the woman who avoids exercise because the effort required is too great or because she doesn't like having to work and push her body. Or it could be a woman who indulges in manicures, pedicures, and massages even when her family struggles financially. In this way, a woman's desire for ease and pleasure governs her life and is her functional god. Comfort can also involve self-soothing through food, or even alcohol and drugs. A woman who uses food for comfort may see food as a reward in good times and solace in hard times. When she feels stressed or sad, she reaches to food as her functional god. Or it may be the woman who spends hours watching television or reading books as a form of escape from the difficulties of life. However it may manifest itself in a woman's life, the underlying motivation of comfort will either lead a woman in one of two directions: to seek comfort in the fleeting things of this world or to seek the enduring comfort only Christ can provide.

CONTROL

Control is the desire to direct things in such a way that the outcome is favorable to you. Fear and a sense of uncertainty are often at the root of a woman's struggle for control. A woman who is concerned with what others think about her may attempt to control their perceptions through a carefully constructed image, never leaving the house without looking her best. Or a woman who struggles to understand and cope with her emotions may seek to gain control through eating and exercise disorders, the use of alcohol or drugs, or even forms of self-injury like cutting or burning. Another woman, ruled by desires to control her family's health and circumstances, may enforce rigid dietary restrictions—buying only organic or non-genetically modified foods and becoming frustrated when her family does not cooperate with her efforts to protect them. She prides herself in being disciplined and responsible. Perhaps she even has her own version of the Ten Commandments, creating rules like "thou shalt run three times a week" and "thou shalt not get two servings of any food. Ever." But her desires to manage and control through her own man-made rules never produces the kind of freedom she is seeking. Instead, she often feels guilty and condemned when she fails to live up to her own expectations, which only leads her to create more performance-based rules. Her desire to control may also extend to others, leaving them feeling frustrated and repressed or constrained by her expectations. When a woman's desire to control her circumstances becomes her functional god, she is refusing to entrust herself to the only one who is in complete control—the Lord who reigns supreme over all the earth and who will work all things together for her good (Romans 8:18–30).

APPROVAL

Approval is being found acceptable in the eyes of another, or when someone holds a favorable opinion of you. Most women want to be recognized, accepted, and valued for who they are. This is not necessarily unhealthy, but all too often, fear of rejection or of not being good enough results in many women becoming enslaved to their desire for approval. This inordinate desire is what drives many young women to succumb to peer pressure or to compromise their integrity in order to fit in with the crowd. A woman who struggles with insecurity and jealousy around other women may seek constant affirmation and assurance from her boyfriend or husband. Similarly, she may struggle to rest secure in her friendships with other women, fearing that they will one day abandon her or leave her out. These insecurities often create tension in her relationships, smothering them and driving a wedge between her and those she values most. This fear of man and need for approval is also why so many women seek compliments, whether through manipulation or through self-deprecating humor. A woman who needs the assurance and approval of others often reaches to something tangible like other people as her functional god; therefore, she is always a slave to those around her, never finding the calming assurance of Jesus' perfect love for her (Romans 8:31–39).

POWER

To be powerful is to have an advantage over another—to get them to do what you want. To be beautiful is to be powerful. Beautiful women are highly praised and valued. Some studies even suggest that those who are considered beautiful are given more opportunities, hired more quickly, and are generally paid more.[5] Beauty is powerful currency with which women are able to secure the affections of suitors, the admiration of others, and command of her surroundings. However, if we peek behind the curtain, we may find that a woman who seeks power is really enslaved to a fear of being powerless or of being humiliated. For some, power is a self-protective covering for deep-seated insecurities. Because she is afraid of looking foolish or being overlooked, a woman with the idol of power may seek to dominate those in her world. She uses her influence in a way that marginalizes the threat others may present. She may do this through her physical appearance, attempting to be the envy of every woman and to have power over men in order to make them do what she wants. She may exercise verbal domination or one-upmanship. Or she may attempt to intimidate others through sculpting six-pack abs and chiseled muscular features. People in her life may feel abused and mistreated. Because she is averse to weakness and vulnerability, she is unwilling to humble herself in complete dependency on the one who alone is all-powerful; therefore, she never enters into the rest of the one who carries her burdens (Matthew 11:28–30).

What we see in all of these underlying motivations is that they are rooted in self-centered fear: fear of suffering, fear of discomfort, fear of sickness and death, fear of being powerless, fear of humiliation and weakness, fear of not being accepted or good enough. The desire for comfort, control, approval, and power are not bad when they find their end in Christ. But rather than taking these fears to the Lord and allowing Him to provide for us in the way He sees fit, we act autonomously, attempting to satisfy ourselves and provide for our own needs. These desires should drive us toward Christ and His all-sufficiency, but instead we run toward the powerless idols that enslave us. But even then the Lord is gracious and compassionate, extending a promise of freedom if we will just return to Him:

> Pay attention, O Jacob, for you are my servant, O Israel. I, the Lord, made you, and I will not forget you.

> I have swept away your sins like a cloud. I have scattered your offenses like the morning mist. Oh, return to me, for I have paid the price to set you free.

> ~ Isaiah 44:21–22 NLT

Rather than deceiving ourselves and desiring to return to the comfort of our slavery, we can turn to the Lord who brings true freedom and security. Everything we desire finds its fulfillment in the Lord. He alone can satisfy the deep longings of our heart.

Questions for Reflection

1. In what ways have you used your body or appearance to get something you desired? Share with the group why you wanted it. Do you feel your motives were pure, impure, or mixed?

2. Have you ever been angry or in despair because you felt you were not "pretty" enough to get something you desired (like a date, spouse, position, or promotion)? How did you deal with this situation? Do you feel your response was justified? Does the group agree or disagree with how you handled the situation?

3. Do you tend to gravitate toward people who you feel will not judge you based on your appearance? What might this reveal about how you deal with your physical insecurities?

4. Of the four main categories of idolatry (comfort, power, control, and approval), which one do you most long for? In what ways is your body image tied to this idol?

SELF-ACCEPTANCE VERSUS GOD'S ACCEPTANCE

French Christian philosopher Blaise Pascal once said there is an infinite abyss within man that can only be filled by an infinite God.[6] When a woman's heart lacks the fullness that a rich relationship with Christ brings, she will eventually seek to fill the abyss in her soul with other things. As this pertains to her body, she may begin to seek identity, significance, security, and acceptance through external rather than spiritual means. **The pursuit of self-esteem and self-acceptance is empty and powerless; it is feeding on ashes.**

Only the acceptance and assurance we find in God is enough to nourish and sustain us. It is the only place we can find safety and rest for our fragile egos. Only God's perfect love can free us from our fears.

> God showed how much he loved us by sending his one and only Son into the world so that we might have eternal life through him. This is real love—not that we loved God, but that he loved us and sent his Son as a sacrifice to take away our sins . . . We know how much God loves us, and we have put our trust in his love . . . God is love, and all who live in love live in God, and God lives in them. And as we live in God, our love grows more perfect. So we will not be afraid on the day of judgment, but we can face him with confidence because we live like Jesus here in this world. Such love has no fear, because perfect love expels all fear.
>
> ~ 1 John 4:9–10, 16–18a NLT

With the perfect love of God as our focus, we can be freed from our endless striving to attain something, and instead operate from the fullness and assurance that is already ours in Christ. God's ever-present, ever-faithful love provides all the comfort, approval, security, and assurance we need. Your acceptance by God is not based on anything you do. It is not based on your performance or your goodness. It is not based on your appearance to Him or to others. It is not even based on how you feel about your appearance. It is based solely on God's character. He paid the ultimate price to set you free.

Because of this we are no longer ruled by our need of people but are free to love them instead. We are freed from the burdens of our need for control and power and set free to live in humble dependence upon an ever-faithful, all-powerful God. With His love for us as our sure foundation, our motivation toward our bodies shifts from empty and self-centered to full and God-centered. When we embrace God's love and acceptance, we are free to forget ourselves and to love others with wild abandon. We can finally pull ourselves away from the reflection in the pool and instead turn our eyes toward others in love and service. *This is the freedom of self-forgetfulness.*[7] And it is available to all who will look to God for their identity, significance, security, and acceptance.

But we must be willing to embrace this by faith—ceasing our laborious pursuit of self-acceptance and self-esteem and instead preaching the truth of God's love and acceptance to our own souls until we believe it and are filled with the truth of His approval and acceptance of us. The choice is ours. Will we accept this precious gift, or will we continue to feed on ashes?

Questions for Reflection

1. What are some ways you seek superficial treatments for your insecurities (fishing for compliments, making fun of yourself, extreme dedication to exercise or dieting, inordinate spending on beauty treatments or clothing)?

2. Who are you trying to encourage with superficial treatment when they really need to find their security in Jesus? How can you help them move toward finding security in Jesus?

3. What might it look like for you to begin to repent (turn) from idolatry surrounding your body image (whether you are allured or repulsed) and find new significance in Jesus?

4. Which is more comforting to you—the approval and acceptance of others or God's approval and acceptance of you? Why? Discuss as a group.

FAITHFUL STEWARDSHIP

WILLPOWER OR WILLINGNESS?

When I was younger, I used to have one particular argument with my dad on a regular basis. I was struggling with a specific sin pattern in my life at the time—doing the same thing over and over again and yet expecting a different result. Every time I came face to face with the consequences of my choices, my dad would say, "You need to be willing to change. Your issue is *willingness*." But I would immediately respond, saying, "No, Dad. It's not an issue of willingness. It's *willpower*, and I don't have any." And so the argument would go—over and over again. It was years later when I realized how wise my dad was about my struggle.

I was caught in a vicious cycle, trying to manage my own life in my own power and in my own way. Over the years, I've noticed the same tendencies in how I care for my body. I have gone through seasons marked by willpower and control, as well as seasons marked by irresponsibility and neglect. Both would leave me paralyzed and unable to move in faith toward God-honoring stewardship of my body.

This kind of unbelief dominates the lives of many women and manifests itself in either **self-righteousness** or **self-condemnation**. Some women may tend toward self-righteousness, and others may tend toward self-condemnation. While still more may, like me, have tendencies to swing from one extreme to the other. The chart below, though not exhaustive, provides some helpful indicators of the unbelief that may be present in our lives regarding our bodies.

Two Kinds of Unbelief

Self-Righteousness	Self-Condemnation
Control	Guilt
Willpower	Shame
Boot-straps mentality	Despair
Rigid Rules	Frustration
Self-Discipline	Neglect/Irresponsibility
Pride/Arrogance	Pride/Insecurity
Judgmental toward others	Judgmental toward self
Inflated sense of identity defined/ based on your body	Deflated sense of identity defined/ based on your body
Hyper-vigilance toward body	Resignation toward body

Trying to navigate the confusion surrounding faithful stewardship of the body is difficult at best because so much of what is prescribed today is self-focused. For a Christian woman, this is especially difficult because the Bible is largely silent with regard to caring for your body. This silence creates tension for many women who want greater clarity than Scripture provides. The temptation then is to read Scripture through our own personal biases, either over-emphasizing or de-emphasizing care of the body.

Our cultural context is vastly different than when the Bible was written, which has produced both opportunities and challenges today that our ancestors did not have. Early readers traveled by foot, labored in fields, made and washed their clothes by hand, hunted and killed their own food, and gathered their own water. Physical needs placed physical demands on their bodies. If they did not physically work to meet those needs, they suffered. But with the technological advances in the thousands of years since the Bible was written, we have been able to be sedentary without suffering. Paul did not need to exhort believers to exercise their bodies because it was part of their everyday life. But this does not mean that Scripture leaves us without direction. If we hope to find freedom from these two forms of unbelief and move toward faithful stewardship of our bodies, we need wisdom.

> If you need wisdom, ask our generous God, and he will give it to you. He will not rebuke you for asking. But when you ask him, be sure that your faith is in God alone. Do not waver, for a person with divided loyalty is as unsettled as a wave of the sea that is blown and tossed by the wind. Such people should not expect to receive anything from the Lord. Their loyalty is divided between God and the world, and they are unstable in everything they do.
>
> ~ James 1:5–8 NLT

There is great hope in this passage. We do not have to be at the mercy of the wind and waves and changing tides of our culture. We do not have to be whipped about by our own divided loyalties or our tendencies toward self-righteousness or self-condemnation. We can instead, in faith, ask our generous God for wisdom and trust that He will provide it. Then, and only then, can we hope to be steadfast and unwavering in how we think, feel, and act toward our bodies.

There is no one solution for every woman. It is much more complex than that. Every woman's body is different and has different needs. Likewise, every season in a woman's life is different, which means that what worked for her in one season of life may not work for her in another season. This means that each woman needs to ask the Lord for wisdom and seek through prayer, through the Scriptures, and through biblical community what it looks like for her to care for her own body in a way that honors God and benefits the greater body of Christ.

Scripture has much to say about the body itself. We were created as physical and spiritual beings, which means that both are good and have value. Jesus died to redeem us, purchasing both our souls as well as our bodies (Colossians 2, 1 Corinthians 15). Having purchased our bodies, He chose to place His Holy Spirit within them as His dwelling place (1 Corinthians 6:19). And though outwardly these bodies are wasting away, they will be resurrected, glorified, and immortal (2 Corinthians 4, 5). Until that day, Paul reminds us that the Lord is for the body and the body is for the Lord (1 Corinthians 6:13); therefore, it matters to the Lord what we do to and with our bodies. And while still in the body, we have work to do—the work of representing Christ to the world.

From creation to re-creation, all of Scripture affirms the value of the body. The Lord created our bodies, Jesus died to redeem them, the Holy Spirit indwells them, and one day these bodies will be resurrected. They have been "stamped as belonging to eternity," destined for resurrection; therefore, they are also for the Lord in the present.[1]

Questions for Reflection

1. Do you tend to struggle more with self-righteousness or self-condemnation regarding your body? How might this reflect unbelief in your life?

2. How have you struggled to care for your body in the past? Do you tend more toward passivity or toward obsession? How has this affected your relationship with others?

3. How might wisdom be important in the faithful care of our bodies?

THE TEMPLE

The wonder and mystery of the temple is that it is where a holy, magnificent God dwells among His people, a place where God and man come together in fellowship reminiscent of Eden. It is the place of His presence, the place where His people worship Him for who He is and what He has done for them. King Solomon built the original temple in all its glory and splendor. But King Nebuchadnezzar destroyed it when he attacked Jerusalem. Those who survived the siege by Babylon were taken captive and remained in Babylon for seventy years. Years later, when Cyrus became King of Persia, the Lord looked with favor upon the Israelites and caused Cyrus to release them so that they might return to Jerusalem and rebuild his temple (Ezra 1). After returning from exile in Babylon, the Israelites began to rebuild the temple, but when they experienced opposition, they abandoned their work, leaving the Lord's dwelling in ruins for many more years (Ezra 2–4).

But in the second year of King Darius' reign, the Lord sent His prophet Haggai with a stern message for the people of Jerusalem:

> Why are you living in luxurious houses while my house lies in ruins? This is what the Lord of Heaven's Armies says: Look at what's happening to you! You have planted much but harvest little. You eat but are not satisfied. You drink but are still thirsty. You put on clothes but cannot keep warm. Your wages disappear as though you were putting them in pockets filled with holes!
>
> ~ Haggai 1:4–6 NLT

The Lord's temple lay in ruin, decaying, while the people of God built fabulous homes for themselves. They abandoned the work He had given them to do and focused instead on their own comfort and satisfaction. But no matter how hard they worked, satisfaction eluded the people of God. Though they built, planted, harvested, and labored, it was all for naught. "They had seed to sow, food to eat, wine to drink, clothes to wear, gainful employment—but no true satisfaction . . . they were not hungry but neither were they satisfied; they were dressed but they were not comfortable." *The people were not experiencing hardship; they were experiencing nonfulfillment.*[2] So the Lord sent them a wake up call through Haggai:

This is what the Lord of Heaven's Armies says: Look at what's happening to you! Now go up into the hills, bring down timber, and rebuild my house. Then I will take pleasure in it and be honored, says the Lord. You hoped for rich harvests, but they were poor. And when you brought your harvest home, I blew it away. Why? Because my house lies in ruins, says the Lord of Heaven's Armies, while all of you are busy building your own fine houses.

~ Haggai 1:7–9 NLT

God's people had lost sight of God's mission. Their focus shifted from working together as the people of God to accomplish the mission of God to that of their own individual pursuits. This isn't unlike what we find among many women today. Women, on the whole, spend excessive time, money, and effort in the pursuit of beauty; even so, satisfaction and contentment remain elusive. Could it be that we, like the Israelites, have lost sight of the mission? Have we neglected the work the Lord has given us to do in building up His temple, and focused our efforts instead on building our own? It could be that we, like the Israelites, need to "consider our ways" (v. 7 ESV).

It is true that our bodies are a temple of the Holy Spirit (1 Corinthians 6:19–20), and therefore, we should care for them. However, *the dominant focus in the New Testament is not on the individual, but on the whole body of believers who make up the temple of the Holy Spirit* (1 Corinthians 3:16–17). Peter calls us "living stones that God is building into his spiritual temple" (1 Peter 2:4–5 NLT). And Paul echoes that when he says that we are "carefully joined together in

[Christ], becoming a holy temple for the Lord . . . being made part of this dwelling where God lives by his Spirit" (Ephesians 2:19–22 NLT). While God is intimately and personally acquainted with each one of us individually (Psalms 139), all throughout Scripture we see God is focused on building a people, a nation, a community of worshipers, into a holy temple where His Spirit can dwell.

This understanding of the temple challenges our individualism, reminding us that we are one people, one body, made up of many parts (1 Corinthians 12). Together we make up the body of Christ. This has both spiritual and physical implications for us.

> Just as our bodies have many parts and each part has a special function, so it is with Christ's body. We are many parts of one body, and we all belong to each other.
>
> ~ Romans 12:4–5 NLT

We all belong to each other, and each member of the body has a special function. This should both humble us and empower us. You are uniquely gifted. You are vital and essential to the body of Christ. However, you are not central to God's plan. *God's plan is not about you; it is about the whole body of Christ.* The gifts you've been given are not for you; they are for others. Even as a married woman, your body does not belong to you but to your husband, and his body belongs to you.[3] But more often than not, this is not how we function. Instead, we neglect the building up of the Lord's temple and focus instead on our own. This thought caused author Marva Dawn to ponder:

"How rarely it is truly understood in the church that we are really all together one Body in Christ, and each member has a different function . . . Imagine what would happen if our congregations truly functioned by means of each person offering his or her gifts to the working together of the whole, if we understood ourselves not so much as individual Christians but as members within the framework of the unity of the Body."[4]

This spiritual reality causes Paul to plead with us to give our physical bodies to God as a living and holy sacrifice in response to all He has done for us (Romans 12:1b NLT). Paul calls this giving of your physical body in service to the Lord your spiritual worship. *Your physical body is inextricably linked to your spiritual worship.* This is critical in our quest for freedom from body-related issues. How you think about your body (whether loathing or loving) and how you treat your body (whether indulging or neglecting), matters to the Lord, and it matters to His church.

Each one of us is a living stone. If one part suffers, the whole suffers. If one part is strong, it helps the others to be strong. My body does not belong to me. It belongs to God and to His church. Your body does not belong to you. It belongs to God and to His church. And God has entrusted us with building His temple, the place for His presence to dwell among us. This should unsettle us and cause us to "consider our ways." The question before us all is this: Whose temple are you building?

Questions for Reflection

1. When you hear the word *temple*, what image comes to mind first (ancient building, your body, or the body of believers)? Which of these three images is the most biblically relevant to you today? Why?

2. Have you ever thought about exercise and the care of your body as something to do for the benefit of the church rather than a benefit for yourself? Is this a new thought for you?

3. Discuss what it might look like for you to be a responsible steward in maintaining your health so that you may serve Christ and His church. How might this affect how much time you spend exercising? Should that time increase or decrease?

FAITHFUL STEWARDSHIP

We were made by God and for God. He created our bodies, and He purchased them through Christ's death and resurrection. He owns our bodies. We are not owners, free to do with them what we please. We are stewards, managers of the body He has given us.

The parable of the talents illustrates the idea of stewardship for us (Matthew 25:14–30). Jesus tells the story of a man going away on a long journey. Before he leaves, the man calls his three servants and entrusts his property to them. He gave to each servant according to his ability. To one servant he gave five talents, to another he gave two, and to the third servant he gave one talent. While the man was on his journey, the servant with five talents invested and made five more. The servant with two talents invested and made two more. But the servant with one talent buried it.

When the master returned, he came to settle his accounts with his servants. When the servant with five talents told him what he had done and gave back to him double what the master had entrusted to him, the master said, "Well done, good and faithful servant. You have been faithful over a little; I will set you over much. Enter into the joy of your master" (v. 21 ESV). Then the servant with two talents told the master what he had done and also gave back to him double what the master had entrusted to him. Again the master said, "Well done, good and faithful servant. You have been faithful over a little; I will set you over much. Enter into the joy of your master" (v. 23 ESV). Finally the servant with one talent approached the master and said, "I was afraid, so I hid your talent in the ground," and with that he gave the master his money back. But this infuriated the master who said, "You wicked and slothful servant! You knew that I reap where I have not sown and gather where I scattered no seed? Then you ought to have invested my money with the bankers, and at my coming I should have received what was my own with interest" (vv. 26-27 ESV). And with that he cast the servant out.

Each servant was given exactly what he needed to do the master's work. The master was pleased with the first two servants because *they were faithful* with what they had been given, *not because of the outcome.* They invested it, used it wisely, and took risks in hopes that it would yield a fruitful return for their master. But the last servant wasted his talent, hiding it in the ground where it could produce no fruit. Whether he was lazy, self-focused, fearful, or indifferent to the master's mission, the truth remains that he had done nothing with what he had been given, and therefore it had benefited no one.

Like the talents entrusted to the servants, your body is something valuable that has been entrusted to you. Your body belongs to the Lord; you are its steward. "A steward is someone entrusted with someone else's property and charged with managing it in the owner's best interest."[5] God has given you great responsibility to care for your body in His best interest. Therefore, stewardship of your body is an act of worship. Faithful stewardship is important not only because God created us, Jesus died for us, and the Spirit indwells us, but also because the body of Christ needs us. **We need to take care of ourselves so that we can fulfill the calling God has for us.**

As women, we have been entrusted with the call of coming alongside others in a way that brings strength and enables them to grow and flourish under our care.[6] Every woman is different and lives out her calling in a variety of ways and in a variety of relationships, but the responsibility is the same. We cannot fulfill our calling if we are *neglecting* our bodies. We also can't live out our callings if we are obsessed with *perfecting* our bodies. Our goal, our mission, is to exercise faithful care of our bodies in a way that enables us to use them in service to God and others, yielding a return that is pleasing to the Master.

We have been created by God for a purpose, and that requires the use of our bodies. Jesus' spiritual ministry demanded physical energy from Him. Likewise, ministering to the needs of others will require physical energy from us as well. We must take care of our bodies as an act of worship and obedience to the God who created, purchased, and indwells them. And we must take care of our bodies as an act of love and service for the body of Christ, our families, friends, and the world around us, as a reflection of the God who loves and cares for His creation. This can be summed up as the greatest commands to love the Lord your God with all your heart, soul, mind, and strength and to love your neighbor as yourself (Mark 12:28–31).

Early in my marriage, my husband urged me to take better care of myself physically. Depending on my mood when the conversation would come up, I would either respond out of insecurity, thinking that he wasn't attracted to me, or I would respond out of arrogance, thinking he was too concerned with physical appearances. Several years later, while having the same conversation, I blurted, "I don't care about loving and taking care of myself. I care about loving and taking care of others." I was comfortable sitting on my spiritual pedestal until he said with all humility, "Taking care of yourself *IS* loving me." In that moment, my hyper-spiritualized view of self-care began to crumble. I knew my husband was right, though it is taking me some time to work out the implications of it in my daily practice.

The undeniable truth is that self-care is important if we are going to be able to care for others. It is why every airline attendant tells you that if tragedy strikes and cabin pressure decreases, you need to put the oxygen mask on yourself before putting one on anyone else. If you pass out, you are no good to anyone. If your body is deteriorating from neglect or abuse, you are not as capable of serving the body of Christ. When you don't maintain a car—taking care to check fluids, change the oil, and put air in the tires—it will eventually stop working. Likewise, if you do not maintain your body—taking care to exercise it and to give it proper nutrients and adequate rest—it will eventually stop working as it should. Both spiritual exercise and physical exercise are important disciplines to your overall wellness. Faithful stewardship of the body, proper self-care, affects you mentally, emotionally, spiritually, and physically. It impacts your overall outlook on life, your confidence, energy level, and mood.

But here is where a word of caution is necessary, where we should again pause to "consider our ways." **Your body is not, first and foremost, an object to be adorned, but an instrument to be used; it is not an end, but a means to an end.** However, this does not mean that you should reject being a source of delight to your husband. On the contrary, God created a woman in such a way that invites the delight of her husband, and this is a good and God-honoring capacity within every woman. It also does not mean that we should reject all superficial treatments like finding fun hairstyles or cute outfits that flatter our figures. Nor does it mean that we cannot enjoy physical exercise simply because it boosts our self-confidence and makes us look better in our clothes. What it does mean is that can't be our sole or even our primary purpose. Taking care of your body solely for appearance purposes is an empty pursuit, and one that will never yield fruit that outlasts us. The Apostle Paul reminded Timothy that "physical training is good, but training for godliness is much better" because it promises "benefits in this life and in the life to come" (1 Timothy 4:8 NLT). Though, at best, our motives will always be mixed, we must continue to remind ourselves that our bodies exist for the Lord and His purposes, and that we exercise and care for them in order to be used by Him and to produce fruit that brings benefits in this life and the life to come.

PURSUING WELLNESS

If we hope to be useful to the Lord, then we must do our part to pursue wellness as an act of worship. This does not mean that every woman needs to train like an Olympic athlete and eat like a rabbit. But it does mean that as a disciple of Jesus Christ, we are to use wisdom, exercise discipline, and be faithful to care for the bodies God has entrusted to us. Though there are some common categories every woman needs to consider, the application of these will look different according to each woman's unique needs, challenges, and seasons of life. What it looks like to be faithful as a single twenty-year-old woman is different from what it looks like to be faithful as a thirty-five-year-old mom with three young children or as a sixty-five-year-old woman. The end goal is not six-pack abs or a bikini-ready body; the goal is wellness—to be healthy in body, mind, and soul in order to be able to better serve the Lord and His people as your spiritual act of worship.

It is important to overall wellness to regularly engage in both spiritual and physical disciplines. There are many important spiritual disciplines such as prayer, solitude, worship, and reading and meditating on Scripture. When a woman exercises her spirit through these disciplines, her faith increases and, as a result, her ability to endure physical challenges increases as well.[7] Similarly, when a woman exercises physical disciplines, it breathes new life and vigor into her spiritually. Both spiritual and physical disciplines work together for the overall good of the body, mind, and soul.

PROPER NOURISHMENT

The body needs proper nourishment if it is to function effectively. The challenge for most women is that there are many differing beliefs about what actually constitutes "proper nourishment." Some believe this is an all vegetarian-based diet, while others believe meat and protein are vital. Others believe that if you can't grow it or raise it, you shouldn't eat it. Yet others believe that any and all food qualifies as nourishment. These differing beliefs over food sometimes even infiltrate the body of Christ, causing members of the body to turn on one another. This should never be so. In fact, Apostle Paul goes into great detail about food being an issue of personal faith and not about rigid man-made restrictions subject to the judgment of others:

> For instance, one person believes it's all right to eat anything. But another believer with a sensitive conscience will eat only vegetables. Those who feel free to eat anything must not look down on those who don't. And those who don't eat certain foods must not condemn those who do, for God has accepted them. Who are you to condemn someone else's servants? Their own master will judge whether they stand or fall. And with the Lord's help, they will stand and receive his approval.
>
> ~ Romans 14:2–4 NLT

Paul goes on to say that the kingdom of God is not about eating and drinking, but about living a life of goodness, peace, and joy in the Holy Spirit (v. 17). And with this in view, Paul says,

> Don't tear apart the work of God over what you eat. Remember, all foods are acceptable, but it is wrong to eat something if it makes another person stumble. It is better not to eat meat or drink wine or do anything else if it might cause another believer to stumble. You may believe there's nothing wrong with what you are doing, but keep it between yourself and God. Blessed are those who don't feel guilty for doing something they have decided is right. But if you have doubts about whether or not you should eat something, you are sinning if you go ahead and do it. For you are not following your convictions. If you do anything you believe is not right, you are sinning.
>
> ~ Roman 14:20–23 NLT

As believers, unity in the body is of utmost importance. We should not allow food to divide us. It is no coincidence that one of the fundamental practices of the Christian faith is that of communion—a shared meal that unites us in fellowship with one another and with God. This meal strengthens and nourishes us spiritually, just as food strengthens and nourishes us physically.

Food is important if we are to remain strong and useful in all seasons and circumstances. To neglect our bodies by starving them or imposing rigid restrictions on them will not only affect us physically, it will affect us spiritually, mentally, and emotionally as well.

Likewise, to indulge our bodies through compulsive eating, continuous overeating, or filling your plate with decadent sugary foods will, over time, harm your overall wellness. It is important to exercise wisdom and self-control, choosing foods that are nutrient rich and portions that are befitting your season, individuality, and circumstances. A college athlete who expends energy in rigorous practices and competitions will need to eat more food than a forty-five-year-old woman who sits behind a desk all day and doesn't exercise often. A woman who is pregnant or nursing requires nourishment not just for her own body but for her baby as well. This means she may need to eat and drink more during this season of her life. Food is important because it is the fuel that keeps the body running well.

But that does not mean that food is for fuel only. Food is also to be enjoyed, to be savored as the God-given gift it is. God gave us taste buds that enable us to identify and enjoy foods that are sweet, salty, or sour. Much has been written in Scripture regarding food and feasting. Jesus performed His first miracle at a wedding feast, making a delicious wine (John 2:1–12). Many spiritual lessons were shared during feasts or over simple meals (John 7, Luke 14). And when Jesus returns we will join together in the wedding feast of the Lamb (Revelation 19:9). The point is that food is a gift of God, to be enjoyed to the glory of God (1 Corinthians 10:31).

The problem for many of us, though, is that food has become our master. As a result, our appetites have gone astray. "It can master us in excessive consumption or in obsessive and fearful nitpicking."[8] As followers of Christ, our attitude toward food should not be one of fear, guilt, or disgust. Nor should we view food as a "necessary evil" or an enemy to slay. Rather, we should receive it humbly, partake of it with thanksgiving—allowing it to strengthen us physically and spiritually—and then offer our bodies back to the Lord in service to Him and the body of Christ.

WORK

The book of Genesis tells us that in the beginning God created the man and the woman in His image and then placed them in the Garden, giving them dominion over it. In essence, they were to tend to the earth, to work it and make it flourish. Though the Lord does not need us, He employs us in the mission to make this world a better place. He calls us to work, to contribute, and to be faithful and diligent. Likewise, the Apostle Paul urges us to never be lazy, but to work hard and serve the Lord enthusiastically (Romans 12:11).

Proverbs 13:4 (ESV) says, "The soul of the sluggard craves and gets nothing, while the soul of the diligent is richly supplied." A sluggard is inactive and lazy, which profits nothing for themselves or for others. On the other hand, a woman who works diligently, whether homeschooling young children, running a non-profit, or selling a product, benefits herself and others. The idea of work is not as much about having an actual job as it is about being a contributor. It's about expending effort and helping further God's mission in this world. The Proverbs 31 woman was a significant contributor to her children, her husband, her servant girls, and to her community, wealthy and poor alike (vv. 20, 23, 28). She was not idle but busied herself in ways that blessed and enriched others (vv. 11–12, 27).

Work looks different according to each woman and her season of life. Physical disabilities may present challenges for some women, but that does not mean they are unable to be a contributor in their own way. One woman may volunteer three days a week to deliver meals to shut-ins, while another may serve at a home for pregnant teenagers. Other women may work a forty-hour work week, while others tutor students in their homes. Even a woman in her later years has valuable time, wisdom, and experience to contribute. For an older woman to spend her retirement years on her own recreation and leisure would be a loss to the entire body of Christ and to her own continued spiritual development.

Hard work, whether physical labor or spiritual labor, is a great teacher. It humbles, challenges, strengthens, and teaches us valuable lessons. There is no shortcut to the spiritual fruit reaped through hard work. It is good for the body, mind, and soul. But are we prepared to labor for God and others? How we care for our bodies now will often determine our capacity to be a contributor in the future.

REST

Rest/sleep is a sign that I trust God to manage without my assistance. (Psalms 3:5–6; 4:8). The Psalmsist says, "It is useless for you to work so hard from early morning until late at night, anxiously working for food to eat; for God gives rest to his loved ones" (Psalms 127:2 NLT). Rest is a gracious gift from the Father to His children. All throughout Scripture we see rhythms of work and rest. When God created the world, He labored for six days. But on the seventh day, the Lord rested (Genesis 2:2–3). Similarly for His people, the Lord instituted that there should be six days of labor and one for rest (Exodus 23:12). He even instituted rest for His creation, granting that mules should have rest from their labor (Exodus 23:12b) and the land have rest from its labor (Exodus 23:10–11). The prophet Elijah, weary from his confrontation with the prophets of Baal, rested under the broom tree while an angel of the Lord ministered to him (1 Kings 19:4–8). Jesus and his disciples stole away from the crowds for rest and renewal (Mark 6:30–31). And Jesus slept; no doubt weary from his labor (Matthew 8:23–24).

Rest, especially sleep, is important for the body, mind, and soul. A Harvard study suggests that proper sleep has a wide-range of benefits. It improves one's memory and ability to learn; aids in regulating the body's metabolism and weight; improves one's mood, reducing irritability and impatience; reduces chances of disease; and increases one's cardiovascular health.[9] Being a faithful steward of your body means giving it the adequate rest it needs in order to be able to function at maximum capacity. This will, of course, be subject to circumstances. The mother of a newborn will lose significant amounts of rest during the first months of her child's life. This is unavoidable. There also may be times that necessitate that you stay up late into the night ministering to someone in need or rejoicing with him or her in times of celebration. To be rigid in the pursuit of proper rest, to the detriment of others, is not being faithful. Nor is it faithful to habitually neglect proper rest. The goal is rest for the purpose of renewal, so that we may be of maximum use to God and others. This means we must create margin in our lives to allow for the rest our bodies need.

RECREATION

Recreation is also important to our renewal. Play is important to the body, mind, and soul. Regular times of fellowship with friends or family breathe fresh life into a weary woman. Studies have shown that when a woman connects relationally with someone through verbal communication, her body releases dopamine and oxytocin, which stimulates the pleasure centers in her brain.[10] Recreation, much like rest, reduces stress, improves your overall outlook, renews your energy, impacts your health, and sharpens your cognitive functions.

Recreation looks different for every woman. For one woman, it may be putting a puzzle together, while for another it may be hiking. Some women may prefer a girls' night out, while others look forward to moments of solitude. For some it may be a good book, and for others it may be playing the guitar. Whatever form of recreation most renews your body, mind, and soul, it is helpful to create margin in your schedule.

Play is not anti-spiritual; the ability to laugh and experience frivolous joy is a rich and gracious gift of God. God-honoring play can be a *response* to joy in the Lord, and it can help *cultivate* joy in the Lord. David danced before the Lord with all his might (2 Samuel 6:5). Zechariah prophesied of the day when young boys and girls would once again fill the streets of Jerusalem, playing and laughing (Zechariah 8:5). And David declared how the Lord turned his mourning into joyful dancing and took away his clothes of mourning and clothed him with joy *that* he might sing praises to the Lord (Psalms

30:11–12, emphasis added). Play better fits you to praise the Lord and to serve others joyfully and with all your might.

EXERCISE

Muscles that are not used will atrophy; that is, they will waste away from their lack of use. It is important that we exercise our bodies, or they will stop working. A body that is weak from disuse cannot serve like a body that has been strengthened through exercise. It would be easy to be distracted by the vanity of our current society and buy into the lie that exercise is all about having the perfect beach body. But this is not the purpose of exercise. The purpose of exercise is to help the body be strong and healthy and function well into our later years. Regular exercise prevents osteoporosis, improves heart and lung conditions, and protects you from developing diseases like cancer and diabetes.[11] But God also created the body in such a magnificent way that regular exercise also increases endorphins that alleviate stress and depression, increases energy, promotes better sleep, and even improves your sex life.[12] The point is that regular exercise promotes an overall sense of wellness in the life of a Christian and may enrich and lengthen the years of your ministry and usefulness to the body of Christ.

There are endless exercise regimens to choose from, so you can choose one that best suits your season of life and personality. Dr. John Dunlop of Johns Hopkins University and author of *Wellness for the Glory of God* suggests that "as little as twenty minutes of exercise a day or 150 minutes a week will help maintain good health."[13] Similarly, the Centers for Disease Control also recommend at least

150 minutes of moderate exercise (brisk walking) or 75 minutes of vigorous exercise (jogging/running) per week, plus two days of a form of muscle strengthening activity such as sit-ups, push-ups, and lunges.[14] Whether you choose to play tennis or lace up your running shoes, strive to exercise your body in a way that helps it remain strong.

As followers of Christ, stewards of the body and the work that has been entrusted to us, we want to strive to faithfully and diligently care for our bodies. All of these disciplines, both physical and spiritual, are vital and make for a healthy body, mind, and soul. But make no mistake; we will not reverse the curse. No efforts at exercise and diet will extend the length of our days beyond what God has appointed for us.

How we faithfully care for our bodies will vary according to each woman and each season of life. Not every season affords the same opportunities. For example, a mother with small children who has only a few energetic hours a day may not have the time, or the energy, to devote to vigorous exercise. For her, faithful stewardship may be placing her children in the stroller and taking them for a walk around the neighborhood or going out in the yard and playing a game of keep away. Or for a woman with chronic pain, faithful stewardship may be going to a pool and swimming or doing water aerobics.

Likewise, a woman who used to suffer from an eating disorder may need to avoid strict diets, while a woman who is overweight and struggles with gluttony may need to seek the accountability and structure a healthy eating plan provides. We will each have propensities toward sin, whether sins of indulgence or sins of neglect, sins of obsession or sins of passivity. We must identify our unique challenges, weaknesses, and temptations. And we must be careful not to compare ourselves to others and hold ourselves to their activity level or hold them to ours. We each need to be responsible to seek through the Scriptures, prayer, and community (which may include a physician) what it looks like for us to faithfully care for our bodies in this season of our lives.

It may not be easy to get started. It may require that we change patterns of thinking and lifelong habits. We might even have to pray for God to give us the willingness to be willing. But we don't need to stand by and wait for God to give us the desire. **Sometimes discipline precedes desire.** We just need to start moving in faith and obedience, making three small wise choices a day, and over a period of years our hearts and our lives will have changed. We must remember our bodies are not the end but the means to an end. They are the means through which we offer ourselves as a living sacrifice to the Lord and in service to one another, in order to help the whole body of Christ grow strong and to bring much glory and praise to God.

Questions for Reflection

1. Have you thought about how physically demanding Jesus' ministry was? How do you think He cared for His body?

2. Imagine Jesus exercising to impress others or overeating to the point that it hindered His ability to walk from town to town and minister. Imagine Him neglecting rest to the point where His mind was not clear enough to teach. Is your care for your body more a reflection of our culture or a

reflection of Jesus? In what ways are you misusing, abusing, or worshiping the body God has given you?

3. After reading this chapter, is your first thought to go on a diet or join a gym? How is that short-sighted? What does good stewardship look like apart from relying on a diet or a gym?

4. In Romans 14:23, Paul said, "Whatever does not proceed from faith is sin." Take a moment to reflect on that statement. Does the way you treat your body—how you eat, dress, exercise, and care for your body—indicate your faith in God and your identity in Christ? Or does it indicate fear, insecurity, or a false sense of power and control? What might it look like to allow faith (and consequentially faithfulness) to govern your choices in self-care?

5. In what ways do you feel you are not being a good steward with your body? What does it look like for you to repent (turn) and move forward in this area? What is one small step you need to take that can begin to turn into a positive habit?

6. What does it look like to manage your body in God's best interest?

6

A WORTHY BEAUTY

I've spent much of my life chasing beauty. It began in middle school. I always felt a little like the ugly duckling—the one who just didn't quite fit in. High school was even worse. The fact that I gained a significant amount of weight in high school didn't help either. I remember when homecoming or pageant nominations would come around. I always secretly hoped my name would be on the ballot—that someone would think I was beautiful enough to nominate me. But it never happened. So with every passing year, I felt more like a failure. I wanted so badly to be desirable, to be the pretty one, to be the one everyone admired. So I did all the things I knew to do to be beautiful. I tried starving myself, but that didn't last long. I teased my hair up to the heavens and caked on the makeup. I tried wearing the right clothes (and the *wrong* ones) and all the new trends. As I became an adult, most of the drama of middle and high school years faded, but my insecurities and desire to be beautiful matured along with me. I spent inordinate amounts of money chasing the ideal, burying myself underneath credit card debt—most of it spent on clothes, shoes, jewelry, makeup. But somehow "it" always eluded me.

It is impossible to talk about body image without addressing appearance, and we can't address appearance without defining and discussing beauty. Many women pursue beauty in varying degrees. For some women, beauty is about a specific size or number on the scale. For others it may be about the right clothing and hairstyles. For others it may be losing excess baby weight, hiding the crow's feet around the eyes, covering up unsightly blemishes, or being the super fit woman. But not every woman chases physical beauty. Some women who feel like they could never be beautiful may have rejected the idea of beauty altogether, swinging to the opposite extreme and doing little to nothing to take care of their physical appearance. Other women may devalue the idea of beauty, thinking it vain and superficial. Still others may see beauty as unimportant and impractical—valuing functionality of the body over its form and appearance. But that does not mean they are not chasing their own version of beauty. For a woman who feels like she could never be considered beautiful, chasing beauty may look more like chasing inner spiritual beauty: seeking to be the best servant or friend or room mom. It may be seeking significance through volunteerism or mothering her children.

I wonder if many of us have stopped long enough to ask ourselves why beauty is so important to us and why we spend so much time and energy chasing it. For me, the desire for beauty was always secondary to a deeper desire. In high school, it was a desire for popularity, to be admired and the center of attention like my beautiful friends. In my twenties and thirties, it was still the desire to be admired, but also the desire to be married, to be desired, and chosen by someone. In my late thirties to early forties, as the aging process began to unfold, I turned more toward the pursuit of spiritual beauty, but my motives weren't entirely pure there either. Deep down there was still a longing to be admired, to be worthy. Whether in middle school or high school, whether pursuing physical or spiritual beauty, beauty was just the currency that would help me get what I wanted. So I pursued it vehemently. **Chasing beauty was a self-centered pursuit to a self-serving end.**

But valuing and cultivating beauty is not the problem. We haven't overvalued beauty in our society; we have undervalued it. We have settled for a definition of beauty that is only skin deep. We need a better understanding of what beauty is and the purpose for which it was created.

For the purpose of this study, we want to define beauty as the essence that attracts or captivates someone's attention. While this does include physical beauty, it is much more than external appearance. Several women come to mind when I think about beauty in these terms. I think of my grandmother who would not have been considered beautiful by today's standards, and yet there was something radiant about her even in her last days. I think about a friend who in her sixties is more vibrant and captivating to me than any woman I know. Or another friend who, though facing significant challenges in her life, displayed strength that was compelling and attractive. I think about a young friend whose vivacious and energetic nature draws me to her like a magnet. These women are *beautiful*, and it has nothing to do with their physical appearance. In fact, I would go so far as to say that their insides transform their outsides, making them far lovelier to me than physical beauty ever could.

Questions for Reflection

1. Do you agree that we have undervalued beauty in our society? If so, how?

2. Is beauty important? Why or why not?

THE PURPOSE OF BEAUTY

But what is the purpose of beauty? Scripture says that *all* things were created by God and for God (Colossians 1:16, John 1:3). And Paul reminds us in the book of Romans that *everything* comes from God, exists by His power, and is intended for His glory (Romans 11:36). **Beauty was created by God, exists by God's power, and its purpose is for God's glory.** This means that God created beauty as a means to attract us to Himself for His own glory. Therefore, we should not despise or reject beauty because it is part of God's creation. But we also should not worship beauty because **the purpose of beauty is to point us to God, who alone is worthy of worship.**

God created each woman distinctly, in His own image. And He has entrusted aspects of His beauty to each woman. Some women may be physically stunning, while others may be spiritually captivating. And God has appointed to each one according to His will, for His glory. Whatever your beauty, whatever the essence God has entrusted to you, your responsibility as a follower of Christ is to be a channel or the means through which God attracts others to Himself. But this requires you to *be willing to be less than what you would like to be if it brings honor and glory to the Lord who made you.* We must decrease so that He can increase (John 3:30).

Unfortunately, many of us would rather be what we aren't and have what we don't. We want the kind of beauty we want, and we want it for our own purposes. So we either reject what God has entrusted to us and chase the beauty of others instead, or, rather than channeling the beauty God entrusted to us and allowing him to shine through us, we capture beauty and make it about us.

Jesus knows our propensity to clean up the outsides—physically and spiritually—to the point that others would admire our beauty, while on the inside we are filled with self-centeredness, bitterness, resentment, entitlement, judgment, dissatisfaction, and discontent. In Matthew 23:27 (NLT), Jesus rebukes the Pharisees and teachers of religious law.

> What sorrow awaits you teachers of religious law and you Pharisees. Hypocrites! For you are like whitewashed tombs—beautiful on the outside but filled on the inside with dead people's bones and all sorts of impurity.

The Pharisees were the religious elite. They were the "spiritually beautiful" of their day. And yet, Jesus rejected their beauty, calling them whitewashed tombs. The language Jesus uses is piercing, calling the Pharisees beautiful on the outside but filled on the inside with death. The Pharisees, those who studied and taught the Lord's law and prided themselves on holiness, had lost sight of what truly mattered. They captured beauty for themselves, seeking glory and honor from one another rather than the honor that comes from God (John 5:44). They lost sight of the truly beautiful and began to pursue lesser things. Can the same be said of us? Have we become so consumed with desire for glory and honor from one another that we are no longer free to draw others to God? Are we so distracted by making the outside beautiful that the insides are rotting away?

CAPTURED BEAUTY

God created beauty to be the essence that attracts someone's attention, drawing others to worship Him and bring Him glory. It is easy to look at a beautiful sunrise or the expansive ocean and be drawn to worship the Creator. The fall season, adorned by a beautiful array of reds, oranges, and yellows, captivates us and again leaves us in awe of the glory of God. Beauty is meant to draw us to God, and when we rightly see and experience beauty, it will culminate in worship. We don't look at the mountains in envy, wishing we were more like them. We don't wish God had created us as beautifully as the sunrise or strive to look more like the peacock with its beautiful crown of feathers. Instead, we look at these things and marvel at the power and majesty of the God who could create such beauty.

But somehow when it comes to the beauty of a woman, we forget the purpose of beauty. Beauty still culminates in worship, but we are worshiping the wrong things. We worship the beautiful woman who ages flawlessly, wanting to be like her. We worship the woman at the gym, who though she's had three kids, still has the perfect body, and we wish we could look like that too. We worship our own strengths, abilities, talents, and beauty. We worship our own self-discipline and health consciousness. We worship the beauty of others and covet it for ourselves, or we dismiss it as irrelevant and worldly. Either way, beauty as we currently understand it is corrupted. But this should not come as a surprise to us. God created beauty; God is the very essence of beauty, and the enemy seeks to destroy all of God's good creation, whether through tempting us to idolize it or to reject it (John 10:10, 1 Peter 5:8, John 8:44). The author Fyodor Dostoyevsky seemed keenly aware of this, stating in his novel *The Brothers Karamazov* that "beauty is mysterious as well as terrible" because "God and the devil are fighting there and the battlefield is the heart of man."[1]

Scripture provides many examples of corrupted beauty. The adulterous woman in the book of Proverbs attracts the attention of onlookers. But rather than being a channel through which God's beauty flows and attracts others, she captures beauty and uses it to draw others in for her own gain (Proverbs 2, 5, 6, 7). She has not only forgotten that God is the source of her beauty, she has also forgotten that the purpose of her beauty is to draw others to God in worship. Or there is the King of Tyre, who was said to be "the model of perfection, full of wisdom and exquisite in beauty" (Ezekiel 28:12 NLT). But his heart was filled with pride because of his beauty and his wisdom was corrupted by his love of splendor (v. 17).

But perhaps the most graphic picture of the corruption of beauty is in the book of Ezekiel. In chapter 16, the prophet Ezekiel recounts the origins of Israel's relationship with Yahweh, their covenant God. He describes Israel as a newborn babe cast aside, naked, unwanted, dumped in a field, kicking about in her own blood, and left to die (vv. 4–6). But the Lord came along and took pity on young Israel, and under His care she grew up and became beautiful (v. 7). He entered into a covenant with Israel, taking her as His bride, giving her expensive clothing, lovely jewelry, and a crown for her head (vv. 10–12). He dressed her in his splendor, and He perfected her beauty (v. 14b). Her fame spread throughout the world because of her beauty (v. 14a), but Israel grew proud and forgot the source of her beauty.

> **"But you thought your fame and beauty were your own.** So you gave yourself as a prostitute to every man who came along. Your beauty was theirs for the asking. You used the lovely things I gave you to make shrines for idols, where you played the prostitute. Unbelievable! How could such a thing ever happen? You took the very jewels and gold and silver ornaments I had given you and made statues of men and worshiped them. This is adultery against me! You used the beautifully embroidered clothes I gave you to dress your idols. Then you used my special oil and my incense to worship them. Imagine it!
>
> ~ Ezekiel 16:15–19a NLT (emphasis mine)

Israel believed her beauty and glory was hers to do with whatever she pleased. So she used it for her own gain.

> On every street corner you defiled your beauty, offering your body to every passerby in an endless stream of prostitution. Then you added lustful Egypt to your lovers, provoking my anger with your increasing promiscuity. That

is why I struck you with my fist and reduced your bound-
aries. I handed you over to your enemies, the Philistines,
and even they were shocked by your lewd conduct. You
have prostituted yourself with the Assyrians, too. It
seems you can never find enough new lovers! And after
your prostitution there, you still were not satisfied. You
added to your lovers by embracing Babylonia, the land of
merchants, but you still weren't satisfied.

~ Ezekiel 16:25–29 NLT

God took the unwanted babe and adorned her with His glory.
He chose her when she was nothing and made her beautiful, desirable. He took her as His own, making her a queen. But Israel took
the beauty entrusted to her by the Lord and used it to secure alli-
ances with pagan nations. One after another, she aligned herself
with nations who were enemies of God, and satisfaction continued
to elude her. No matter what, it was not enough—not enough power,
not enough fame, not enough security. Israel was not content in her
identity as the bride of Yahweh, to which the Lord responded, "Yes,
you are an adulterous wife who takes in strangers instead of her own
husband" (Ezekiel 16:32 NLT).

Israel used what God *had* entrusted to her to pursue that which
He *had not* given her. Rather than delighting in who the Lord created
her to be and enjoying her covenant relationship with Him and trusting Him, she turned her back on Him and instead sought to make
herself great. But what are the spiritual implications of this passage
for a woman when it comes to beauty? God was the source of Israel's

beauty. He chose her. He created her. He gave her an identity. But she rejected that and sought to create her own identity instead. Likewise, God chose you. He created you and gave you an identity that is unique to you. This brings Him much glory. But are you, like Israel, rejecting who God created you to be and pursuing instead your own identity? Are you seeking the praise of strangers instead of your God?

Consider two women: one is attractive by cultural standards and admired for her beauty. The other woman, while not necessarily physically attractive, is admired for her spirituality. Both women have a choice to make. Will they capture the admiration of others for themselves, or will they hold it loosely, giving glory to God alone? *Whether we are chasing physical beauty or spiritual beauty, the question we need to ask ourselves is this: whose glory are we seeking? Is our desire for beauty, whether spiritual or physical, self-serving?*

CHANNELED BEAUTY

In today's culture, it is hard to even imagine what it might look like to embody or channel true, God-honoring beauty. But we are not without example. Jesus, who is the visible image of the invisible God and the One in whom all the fullness of God was pleased to dwell (Colossians 1:15–20), is our example of the embodied, channeled beauty of God. But what does the beauty of God look like through the embodied Christ? The prophet Isaiah tells us that there was nothing "beautiful or majestic about his appearance, nothing to attract us to him" (Isaiah 53:2b NLT). There was nothing impressive about Jesus—at least, not to the physical eye. There was nothing about Him that would draw us to Him. Unlike King Saul and King Solomon, who were regal and stately, or the King of Tyre, who was exquisite in beauty, Jesus was a mere carpenter's son from the unimpressive town of Nazareth.

But Jesus was no mere man. He was fully God and fully man. If anyone had reason to boast, if anyone had reason to pursue His own glory, it was Jesus. If anyone deserved praise, it was Jesus. But even though He was God, He did not count equality with God as something to be grasped. Instead, Jesus "emptied himself, by taking the form of a servant" (Philippians 2:6–7 ESV). Israel used her God-given privilege to exalt herself, but Jesus exalted the Father. Even when others believed in Him and praised Him, Jesus would not entrust Himself to them, because He knew their hearts; He knew that even the praise of man is often fickle and self-serving (John 2:24).

This attitude of humility and servanthood is what defined Jesus' personal ministry while on earth. This freed Him to bring glory to God, rather than seek it for Himself. He was not dependent upon what others thought of Him. He was not destroyed and despairing when they rejected Him. This is not to say that He didn't experience joy and pain. On the contrary, because Jesus was fully man, he experienced heartbreak, betrayal, abandonment, sorrow, and agony (Isaiah 53:3b, John 11:35, Matthew 27:46, Luke 22:44). He was not callous and unfeeling; He was steadfast and faithful because rather than looking to others for approval, He looked to God alone.

Though Jesus was despised and rejected, he did not waver. He washed the feet of His companions, even those He knew would betray and abandon Him (John 13). He carried our weaknesses (Isaiah 53:4a);

was pierced for our rebellion and crushed for our sins; and was beaten so we could be whole and whipped so we could be healed (Isaiah 53:5). He was oppressed and treated harshly (Isaiah 53:7a), stripped, mocked, spit on (Matthew 27:27–31). Throughout His life, Jesus did not defend Himself or seek His own glory and honor. He rejected the temptation to provide for Himself or to exalt Himself (Matthew 4:1–11). Ultimately, He humbled Himself in obedience to God and died a criminal's death on the cross (Phil. 2:8). And the Lord said that because of Christ's experience, because of His **self-abandonment**, He made it possible for many to be counted righteous because He bore all their sins (Isaiah 53:11b). Contrary to Israel, who prostituted her God-given beauty to the surrounding nations and was never satisfied, when Jesus looks on all that is accomplished through the giving over of His body, He is satisfied (Isaiah 53:11a).

God created everything through Christ, including beauty (Colossians 1:16–17). But even though Jesus is the source of beauty, he captured no glory for Himself. Instead, He allowed the beauty of the Father to flow through Him so that others may be drawn into relationship with God. The beauty of God is visible in the outstretched arms of Christ on the cross—His body bloodied, pierced, striped, exhausted, and spent. The beauty of God is visible in the blood that flowed from Jesus' side as He hung upon the cross. There is nothing that should physically attract us to a bloodied body hanging upon a cross. Yet we stand at the foot of the cross, awestruck and worshipful, because of God's beautifully redemptive plan to bring us back to Himself. *This beauty is not self-serving; it is self-giving.* It is a blessing to others.

Likewise, God's beauty channeled through a woman is selfless and sacrificial. It is *self-abandoning* and *self-forgetting*. A woman who is freed from obsessive pursuits for beauty isn't concerned with trying to impress others, whether through physical beauty or impressive spirituality. She isn't consumed with her flaws and imperfections. She doesn't seek praise and adoration, but she can receive it graciously and humbly because she recognizes God as both its source and purpose.

Ultimately, beauty is a blessing to others. **But if you desire to channel the beauty of God, you must seek peace with what you aren't in order to be the best of what you are**. The Proverbs 31 woman is praised not for her charm or her beauty, but for her fear of the Lord and her self-abandonment and service to others. The beauty she displays is sacrificial – rising early in the morning and working late into the night. Likely she wears the visible signs of labor on her body. But she is beautiful. The woman in 1 Peter 3 is not considered beautiful because of the way she adorns her body, but for the way she trusts God and honors her husband. Because she entrusts herself to the Lord, she does not need to self-protect or self-promote. She instead adorns herself with a gentle strength and a quiet assuredness that may be a blessing to her husband, winning him to Christ through her actions (1 Peter 3:1–6). Paul encouraged the women of God to make themselves attractive not so much through their physical appearance as through the good things they do (1 Timothy 2:10).

God's beauty is displayed through the woman whose breasts sag because she nursed her children, allowing them to draw life from her body. It's present in the woman whose hands are arthritic from years of handwritten notes to people in need of encouragement. It's visible through the young girl who chooses to wear non-name brand clothes so that she may give more to those who are in need. It's channeled through the woman with bags under her eyes because she stayed up late caring for a friend. It's evidenced in the woman who rises early to exercise her body each day so that she is able to keep up with her grandchildren and in the calloused hands of the woman who tends to her elderly neighbor's yard. It's displayed through the smile lines from the joy and laughter experienced in fellowship with others. And it is visible in the dirty, calloused feet of those who bring the good news of Christ to others (Romans 10:15, Isaiah 52:7).

The Psalmsist wrote, "From Mount Zion, the perfection of beauty, God shines in glorious radiance" (Psalms 50:2 NLT). In the Psalmsist's days, Mount Zion was the city of David, the place where God's presence dwelled among His people. It was the place where heaven and earth intersected. But today, God's presence is no longer confined to one place. Instead, God dwells in and among His people, the body of Christ. We are now the place where heaven and earth intersect. This is significant. **The perfection of beauty is God's presence in God's people as they together live their lives in service to God and one another.** And when we do that, God shines forth in glorious radiance.

Channeling the perfect beauty of the Lord is spending our lives in service to others. It is to give of our bodies in a way that marks us, just as Christ is marked. And it is rejoicing that the Lord would allow us to reflect Christ in the marks we bear on our bodies. It does not mean that we do not take care of ourselves, nor does it mean that we can't enjoy cute clothes, fun nail colors, or a trendy hairstyle. But it does mean that we do not place our identity in beauty, whether physical or spiritual. Rather, we channel the perfect beauty of God's presence in humble servitude and pouring ourselves out for others. It means we spend more time adorning ourselves with the character of Christ—with forgiveness, patience, love, kindness, compassion, thankfulness, and humility (Colossians 3:12–15) **so that** we may draw others to know Christ and be changed by Him. It's pursuing Christ's fame, glory, and honor instead of our own. It's looking to the Lord and reminding yourself daily of who God is and all He has done for you in Christ so that you are free to be a vessel of His goodness and mercy to the world. **It is seeking peace with what you aren't in order to be the best of what you are.** As the Psalmsist said, "Those who look to him are radiant, and their faces shall never be ashamed" (Psalms 34:5 ESV).

The question before us is this: will we look to Him and allow His beauty to flow through us? Will we, as the place where heaven and earth intersect, allow the perfection of God's beauty to shine forth so that others may be drawn to Him? Or will we try to capture beauty for ourselves? What will you do with the beauty God has given you?

Questions for Reflection

1. Circle the words you feel more accurately describe how you think about beauty. Discuss why you circled what you did.
   Decorative or Useful
   Channeled or Captured
   Reflective or Alluring

2. At the beginning of this study, we asked you to define beauty. How has your perspective changed? Have you been thinking of beauty from more of a cultural perspective or a biblical perspective? How are they different?

3. What is the purpose of beauty? Why do you think God created it?

4. Read Isaiah 53 aloud in your group. Was Jesus beautiful? Discuss as a group.

5. In what ways have you captured beauty for yourself instead of channeling it to bring glory to God? What does it look like for you to repent (turn) in this area?

6. What is one practical thing you need to stop or start doing in order to use the beauty God has given you to bring glory to Him?

7. What is something you need to make peace with in order to become the best of what you are?

8. What do you think it means to have a worthy beauty?

CULTIVATING A THANKFUL HEART

HUMAN DESIRE

"If I could just lose five pounds . . ." Words I've uttered countless times over the course of my life. For many years I believed I would be satisfied *when* I shed the extra baggage. And I was right to a certain extent. I did need to shed some extra baggage. But the baggage I was carrying was not those five extra pounds; *it was instead the idea that my internal satisfaction was tied to my external circumstances.* That idea kept me tethered to my circumstances and dependent on outcomes, rather than helping me find freedom from them.

My problem was that I believed that satisfaction could be found in the next goal, the next possession, the next accolade. But time and experience have proven that is not the case. Eventually I would lose those five pounds, only to hear myself say, "Just five more . . ." The truth is that whenever I attained "the thing" I'd set my sights on, I found a "new thing" to take its place. And then the process would begin all over again—satisfaction always eluding me. Whatever I felt

I lacked is where I set my gaze and what became the object of my desire. Most of these desires were good things, reasonable things. I wanted to be married, to have a family, to have a job that enabled me to support myself, a college degree. Some of the things I desired were within my control, and some were not. But none of them (at the time) were a part of my current circumstances. Rather than being focused on God's current provision, I was focused on what I didn't have. And if I allowed that to continue for too long, I even grew disenchanted with what I did have.

Eve had the same problem. She was surrounded by the abundance of the Garden. It was beautiful and bountiful, and she lacked no good thing. But as soon as the serpent directed her gaze to the forbidden fruit, telling her that it would make her like God, knowing both good and evil, she began to crave it (Genesis 3:4). She wanted the wisdom it would give her; she wanted to be like God. Both of these desires seem reasonable enough, like worthy pursuits. But as the serpent "dangled the carrot" before her eyes, Eve grew discontent. She wanted more, better, different than what she had. She began to believe that what the serpent offered her held more promise, more joy, more good than what God had provided. She was no longer satisfied to be who she was—a creature dependent upon God—and to trust in how God had created her, limited in wisdom and understanding. She aspired to something she perceived as greater, and so she reached for "the thing" that would help her attain it.

"Human desire is never satisfied" (Proverbs 27:20 NLT). The well of human desire is bottomless, never sated and always seeking something upon which to feed itself. Charles Spurgeon once said, "You say, 'If I had a little more I would be very well satisfied.' You make a mistake: if you are not content with what you have, you would not be satisfied if it were doubled."[1] This is a spiritual problem of great magnitude, because **an unsatisfied heart is easily deceived.** It's me believing that satisfaction could be found in losing five more pounds. It's Eve believing that the fruit would bring fulfillment. It's the woman who gets cosmetic surgery thinking that she will finally be content with her appearance. It's the young girl who believes the latest trend in women's fashion will help her fit in with her peers.

The result of our insatiable hunger is that we become slaves to our desires, to the lust of our eyes. This makes us vulnerable to the deception of the world, our own flesh, and the devil. The serpent dangles the carrot in front of us whispering reasonable sounding arguments:

"It's your body. You should be able to do whatever you want with it."

"You're going to die of something. You might as well enjoy this life while it lasts."

"Your body is a temple. It's only right that you would spend so much time and money to take care of it."

"So what if you are fifty pounds overweight?! People are too focused on outward appearance. It's your heart that matters."

Statements like these are rampant in today's society. Some of them even have partial truths within them, which makes them seem all the more reasonable. Pastor R. Kent Hughes warns of this kind of deception, saying, "There are enticing voices all around . . . and some of what they say sounds logical . . . Deception looks authentic. It is supported by intelligence, credentials, popularity, even a touch of class."[2] Some of these deceptive arguments may come through the well intentioned but misguided efforts of your own doctors, spiritual leaders, peers, or family. Others may come through the book you're reading or the television show you're watching. Some of them are even the result of your own efforts to justify and rationalize your craving. More often than not, all of these arguments point you back to your own rights to happiness and personal autonomy. And therein lies the danger for all of us, as Dennis Kinlaw explains:

"Satan disguises himself under the ruse of personal autonomy. He never asks us to become his servants. Never once did the serpent say to Eve, 'I want to be your master.' The shift in commitment is never from Christ to evil; it is always from Christ to self. And instead of His will, self-interest now rules and what I want reigns."[3]

Most people, especially those who follow Christ, would rarely choose evil knowingly. That is not to say that most, if not all, of us have not chosen to act in willful rebellion at some point in time. But more often than not, most people would not choose evil. Deception is much more subtle than that, or we would not be easily deceived. More often than not, the choice is not between good and evil; it is between God and self. It's what happened to Eve in the Garden. And it is what happens to us where our bodies are concerned. The discontent dwelling in the hidden crevices of our hearts leaves us easy prey to our own desires and the deceptions of this world and Satan. And unless we are armed and ready, we may find that we reach again for the fruit.

DISCONTENTED GRUMBLERS

We find a great example of this in the books of Exodus and Numbers. The Israelites, God's chosen people, lived in Egypt for 430 years (Exodus 12:41), much of it under brutal slavery. The Lord, remembering His covenant with Abraham, Isaac, and Jacob, sent a man named Moses to deliver Israel out of their slavery and into the abundance of the Promised Land (Exodus 3:16–17). The Lord delivered the Israelites from their enemies in such a miraculous way that their Egyptian captors not only freed them but also gave them whatever the Israelites asked for—including silver, gold, and clothing (Exodus 12:35–36). His very presence led them out of Egypt in a cloud by day and fire by night (Exodus 13:21-22). And when their enemies decided to pursue them, the Lord swallowed them up in the Red Sea (Exodus 14).

It is evident that God was with the Israelites, protecting them from harm and providing for their needs. But fresh on the heels of their miraculous deliverance, they encounter their first hardship—they were thirsty and without water for three days, and when they finally found water, it was so bitter they couldn't drink it. But Moses, at the Lord's direction, throws a piece of wood in the water, and the water becomes sweet. Then Moses leads the people to Elim, a place with twelve springs and seventy palm trees, and they set up camp

(Exodus 15:22–27). Thus far the Lord has provided for the Israelites in miraculous ways, but now as they move on from Elim into the wilderness of Sin (Exodus 16:1), they are hungry. And once again the Lord provides, raining down bread and quail from heaven (Exodus 16:4–5). Every morning the Lord provided the bread (manna) from heaven so that everyone may collect as much as they need for their family. Day in and day out, the manna appeared and the people of Israel ate and had their fill. Then, at the Lord's command, the people journey to Rephidim, where they again grow thirsty, and once again the Lord provides (Exodus 17:1–7).

The Israelites wanted water. They wanted food. They wanted meat (Numbers 11:4–6). These are reasonable, understandable desires for the most basic needs. At first glance it is hard to blame them for their reactions. But if we look more closely, we see a pattern that emerges all throughout the books of Exodus and Numbers.

Fresh out of slavery in Egypt—*they grumbled* (Exodus 14:10–12). Fed with bread from heaven—*they grumbled*. Longing for the foods they had in Egypt—*they grumbled* (Exodus 16:3, Numbers 11:4–6). They wanted meat so badly, in fact, that they would have rather remained enslaved in Egypt and been killed. Hearing from the spies who had scouted out the abundant Promised Land—*they grumbled* (Numbers 13:25–14:4). The problem was not the hardship they endured, nor the "inadequate" provisions of God. The Israelites were their own problem. No matter what they had, they wanted more, better, different. Rather than being thankful for the way the Lord was providing for them and trusting Him, they were frustrated and dissatisfied. Nothing was ever enough. The Israelites had a chronic problem—they were **discontented grumblers**.

The word *grumble*, in the original Hebrew, means to make ill-natured complaints in a low voice, to mutter with discontent.[4] **A grumbler is a person with a discontented disposition.** In his book *The Practice of Godliness*, Jerry Bridges says that the "very first temptation in the history of mankind was the temptation to be discontent."[5] He goes on to say that discontentment is to question the goodness of God. This is exactly what we see of Eve in the Garden of Eden and of the Israelites as they traveled through the desert. And it is the same problem that we have as women navigating a world that idolizes the body and physical beauty. We are discontented grumblers, never satisfied with the provision of the Lord. We want more, better, different. We feel slighted and want what we don't have. We cry out to God, whether through our words, thoughts, or actions, "Why did you make me this way?" (Romans 9:20 NLT). We long for the stretch-mark-free days before children. We crave the days of our youth.

In Luke 6:44–45, Jesus talked about a tree and its fruit—a good tree produces good fruit and a bad tree produces bad fruit. He concluded by saying that "what you say flows from what is in your heart." If you listen to women talk for a while, it is easy to pick up the verbal cues of discontent emanating from our hearts. Cues like "I wish I . . ." or "If I didn't have . . ." and even "If I could just . . ." are often uttered at least once during a conversation. It is also apparent in our English language through the comparative adjectives we use—words like *prettier, taller, funnier, trendier,* or *skinnier.* The very idea of these words means we are comparing two things and determining that one has more value over another. *The grumblings of our mouths expose the discontent of our hearts.*

Grumbling is a luxury the Christian woman cannot afford—not if she wants to grow in maturity as a follower of Christ. We must not be deceived; we will reap what we sow. *If we sow grumbling, we will harvest discontent, dis-ease, and bitterness.* Grumbling slowly and silently poisons our faith. As our belief in the goodness of God wanes, we become easy prey to the temptations of our own flesh and those of the devil. We are easily deceived into believing there is something better and that what God has provided is not enough. This hinders our effectiveness in the kingdom because "resentment of what we don't have is the number one reason we don't use what we do have."[6] The end result of our discontented grumbling is autonomy; we reach for "the thing" we think will satisfy us. We step outside of God's *good* provision and reach for what we have judged as "better" or more desirable. Eve reached for the apple. The Israelites desired to return to Egypt, to the land of their slavery. And we reach for food, exercise, cosmetic surgery, gym memberships, or the next fashion trend.

Grumbling also spreads among the community. It is a contagious disease—one grumbler inciting grumbling in another (Numbers 11:4, Numbers 13:25–14:4). Women commiserate with one another over their perceived flaws, often as a way of relating to one another without recognizing the dangers of it. At the very least, it perpetuates the cycle of grumbling in the community. One woman complaining about her body can also create confusion and insecurity in another woman, causing her to begin to question her beliefs about her own body. And at worst, it calls the goodness of God into question and robs Him of the worship and thanksgiving due Him.

Ultimately, and possibly most importantly, grumbling is failure to be thankful for what God has provided. More often than not, people *feel* thankful as a response to some external stimuli, some kindness or blessing received. And this is a right response. But thankfulness is not just a feeling; it is not just passive. **Thankfulness is active; it must be cultivated, maintained, fed**. Again, we reap what we sow. *If we sow thankfulness, we will reap wholeness, contentment, and peace.*

Paul encouraged this in the book of 1 Thessalonians: *"give thanks in all circumstances; for this is the will of God in Christ Jesus for you"* (1 Thessalonians 5:18 ESV, emphasis added). Thankfulness, according to Paul, is not a response to our circumstances; it is a deliberate act of the will. Paul suffered greatly. He was imprisoned, and he endured beatings and many hardships. He went without food, without rest, and endured a thorn in his flesh, and yet he worshiped *in* prison and gave thanks in all circumstances. There is no doubt that he suffered greatly. It would be easy to think of Paul as superhuman or having some capacity that eludes us. But Paul was not superhuman; he was an ordinary man. He was thankful because he knew who he was; apart from Christ, he was the worst of sinners (1 Timothy 1:15). And he was thankful because he knew who he was in Christ—loved, chosen, adopted, forgiven, holy, and without fault (Ephesians 1:3–8). Paul knew that in Christ, God had already met his greatest need: the forgiveness of sin and restoration of a relationship with God. And it was from this knowledge that he gave thanks in all things. And his thankfulness was magnetic. As a result of Paul's steadfast faith and thankfulness, even one of his jailers (as well as the jailer's entire family) came to know Christ (Acts 16:16–34).

Thankfulness is God's will for us as Christ followers (1 Thessalonians 5:18). Therefore, it is vital to our spiritual maturity, and it is vital to the body of Christ.

CHARACTERISTICS OF A THANKFUL HEART

Many women struggle to *feel* thankful for their bodies for a variety of reasons. For one woman, it may be the disease that is ravaging her body. For another, it may be the deterioration brought on by age. While for another, it may be the weight she's gained as the result of some medicine she is taking. For yet another, it may be the failure to measure up to the standard of beauty in her cultural context. Whatever the circumstance, feeling thankful is hard. But feelings aren't facts, and therefore they do not need to dictate our actions. Our call as Christians is to submit our bodies to Christ by *giving thanks* in all things.

When a woman gives thanks in all things, she is **humble** (Psalms 103, Philippians 2:1–11). She understands that she is wholly dependent on God for life. Every breath of her lungs, every beat of her heart has been given to her by the Creator and Sustainer of life. A humble woman is fully dependent on the Lord, submitting herself to the "power and will of God." She does not have a sense of entitlement because she has a modest opinion of herself. Rather than seeking to exalt herself through perfecting her body, she exalts the Lord as the source of all life, meaning, value, and significance.

A woman who gives thanks in all things is **reverent** (Psalms 111). She recognizes that her body was created by God and for God, and that God purchased it at the high price of Jesus' blood shed on the cross for her. She understands that her body does not belong to her but has been entrusted to her care and management to do good works. Because she respects God as her Lord and King, she treats her body with respect. She does not abuse it, mistreat it, indulge it, hate it, neglect it, or become obsessed with it. Instead, she cares for it as His instrument and offers it back to Him as a living sacrifice (Romans 12:1).

A woman with a thankful heart is **steadfast** (Colossians 2:6–7). Her joy, her faith in God's goodness, and her thankfulness are not dependent on outside circumstances. She is not easily swayed by others' opinions, empty promises, the allure of the world, or her own desires. She is firmly rooted in the truth of God's Word, in who God is, and in who she is in Christ. Her steadfastness is indicative of the growing, abundant, vital relationship she has with Jesus Christ. She follows Christ's example, trusting in God's provision in the face of weakness and temptation; therefore, she is able to resist the temptations of the devil and the cravings of her own flesh (Matthew 4:1–11).

A woman who gives thanks in all things is also **wise** (Psalms 42, 43, and 90). Thankfulness is not naive. It is not sticking one's head in the sand and ignoring external circumstances. A wise woman is not ignorant or blind to need, trouble, suffering, or strife. On the contrary, she understands that the world she lives in is broken and riddled with suffering. She sees it all around her, and she has experienced it herself in many ways. Yet she is able to praise the Lord in the midst of her suffering. She understands that she is finite and frail. She knows and believes that everything she experiences is under His gracious and sovereign Lordship, and is therefore able to accept all things, both good and bad, from his hand. She is able, like Job, to say, "Though he slay me, I will hope in him" (Job 13:15a NLT).

A woman who cultivates thankfulness is **content** (Psalms 23). She is not anxious, frustrated, resentful, bitter, or worried over the body that has been entrusted to her. She does not endlessly strive to perfect herself, but she does seek to be a good steward of her body. She does not bemoan what she doesn't have, nor does she indulge in endless gratification of her desires. She is also not apathetic, resigned, or complacent toward her body. Rather, she has learned how to be content in every circumstance, whether ignored and mocked or praised and adored, whether in abundance or in need, in plenty or in want, in weakness or in strength (Philippians 4:11–13). She believes that what God has given her is *enough; it is sufficient,* and she therefore receives it from Him humbly, with thanksgiving.

Finally, a woman who sows thankfulness is **worshipful** (Psalms 95, 107). To give thanks to the Lord is to praise the Lord for who He is and all He has done. Choosing to give thanks, regardless of circumstances, is choosing to acknowledge the goodness of the Lord and to praise His great name. Thanksgiving is worship. By failing to give thanks for our bodies, regardless of their state, we deny the Lord praise due Him. But choosing to thank the Lord in all seasons and circumstances is a thanks offering pleasing to the Lord.

CULTIVATING A THANKFUL HEART

So what must we do to cultivate a thankful heart? Though it is simple, it is in no way easy. It requires intentional effort on our part, taking every thought captive and making it obedient to Christ (2 Corinthians 10:5). This means we must examine our thoughts about our bodies. What do you think and feel when you think about your body? Are you frustrated and despising of it? Are you obsessed with caring for it? Wherever we find our thoughts wandering during the day, we would be wise to heed Paul's encouragement to the Philippians: *"Fix your thoughts* on what is <u>true</u>, and <u>honorable</u>, and <u>right</u>, and <u>pure</u>, and <u>lovely</u>, and <u>admirable</u>. *Think about things* that are <u>excellent</u> and <u>worthy of praise</u>" (Philippians 4:8 NLT, emphasis mine).

Cultivating a thankful heart means focusing our minds, our thoughts on things that are excellent and worthy of praise. A woman who desires to cultivate a thankful heart will **reflect on God's past faithfulness and provision**. Dale Ralph Davis, author of many biblical commentaries, says that "memory . . . keeps gratitude fresh and . . . gratitude keeps faith fruitful."[7] As one body of Christ, we look all the way back to Genesis 3 when the Lord promised to send one who would conquer sin and death once and for all, making a way for His people to be restored to Him for all eternity. That promise was fully and finally fulfilled in the life, death, and resurrection of Jesus Christ. The body of Christ has many reasons to praise God for His past faithfulness and provision.

But we can also look back over our own personal lives and see how God has been faithful. Whether it is drawing you into a personal relationship with Him, protecting you from the illness that threatened your life and vitality, or helping you persevere in the face of adversity, God has been faithful. If you are going to cultivate a thankful heart, you must daily reflect on God's past faithfulness and provision, lest you forget and be tempted to fear and despair. Whether through journaling or creating gratitude lists, we should strive to be like Samuel, who looked back over God's faithfulness and provision and declared, "Thus far the Lord has helped us" (1 Samuel 7:12 NIV).

Cultivating a thankful heart also means we **acknowledge God's present provision**. Corporately, God's Spirit is with us—growing and sustaining the church as the body of Christ. But personally, His Spirit is also present with us. If we draw breath, it is from Him. If our heart continues to beat, it is because He causes it to do so. All things are from Him, through Him, and for Him (Romans 11:36). If you survey the landscape of your life, what do you see that God has provided? If you are able to see, hear, taste, smell, and feel, those are reasons to thank Him. Are you relatively healthy? Are your basic needs met? Thank Him. It may be that we have grown so accustomed to the blessings of our life that we have begun to take them for granted, treating them as rights instead of the good, gracious gifts they are. Acknowledging God's present provision requires faith and eyes to see. If you struggle to see how God is active and present in your life, pray that He would open your eyes to the ways in which He daily provides for you. He has not promised to give us everything we want. But He does give us what we need, and that is sufficient.

Cultivating a thankful heart also means that we **look forward with assurance** to the fulfillment of God's promises to us. While we look back at God's past faithfulness in providing Christ as a sacrifice for our sin, and His current faithfulness in His commitment to Christ's bride—the church—we also look forward to the day that Christ returns for His bride and ushers in His kingdom. We look forward with great anticipation to the Lord fulfilling His promise that He will one day make everything in heaven and on earth new. Personally, we look forward to a day when we will stand before God, whole and complete. Your body will no longer be subject to death, disease, decay, or suffering. The body we now inhabit will die and be buried, but it will be raised to live forever. It will be buried in brokenness but raised in glory. It will be buried in weakness but raised in strength (1 Corinthians 15:42–43). This is the day we look forward to—the day when God fulfills His promise to make all things new.

Questions for Reflection

1. When do you last remember "grumbling" or complaining about your body? When was the last time you heard another woman "grumble" about her body? How did you respond to her grumbling?

2. If Jesus were still walking the earth and you encountered Him, what would you say to Him regarding the way He made you? Is your first thought thankfulness or discontent?

3. Read James 4:1–10 aloud in your group. When you think

about your body, is there anything that makes you angry because God has not given it to you? Why do you desire it? Is there a way you think you might be chasing your own desires instead of what Jesus may desire for you?

4. If discontentment leads to deception, what is one way you may be deceived in how you are using your body or thinking about it?

5. How often is your internal satisfaction tied to your external circumstances? How might this need to change? What is one step you can take to begin to cultivate a thankful heart?

6. In what ways have you learned contentment with the body God has given you?

SHINING BRIGHT

Cultivating thankfulness is spiritual discipline that is important to the body of Christ. The Apostle Paul challenges us to do all things without grumbling and disputing so that no one can criticize us, and to live clean, innocent lives as children of God, "shining like bright lights in a world full of crooked and perverse people" (Philippians 2:14–16 NLT). When we live without grumbling and complaining, we are able to shine as lights in a lost and dark world that needs the hope that only Christ can provide. We cannot be effective ministers of the abundant, joyful life in Christ if our speech is full of complaining. A thankful spirit is good for the body of Christ and for those who have yet to find Christ.

Cultivating a thankful heart is also important to our own body. Again in the book of Philippians, Paul says,

Always be full of joy in the Lord. I say it again—rejoice!
Let everyone see that you are considerate in all you do.
Remember, the Lord is coming soon. Don't worry about
anything; instead, pray about everything. Tell God what
you need, and thank him for all he has done. **Then you will
experience God's peace**, which exceeds anything we can
understand. His peace will guard your hearts and minds as
you live in Christ Jesus.

~ Philippians 4:4-7 NLT (emphasis mine)

Finding our joy in Christ, trusting in His faithfulness and provision, and thanking Him for all He has done (including making and sustaining our bodies) brings God's peace—a peace that exceeds anything we can understand. This is not naïve thankfulness. It is thankfulness built solidly on the rock of Jesus Christ. Thankfulness is a path to peace, and a heart of peace gives fullness of life to the body (Proverbs 14:30). Let's follow the example of 17th century poet George Herbert who wrote:

Thou that hast giv'n so much to me,

Give one thing more, a gratefull heart . . .

Not thankfull, when it pleaseth me;

As if thy blessings had spare dayes:

But such a heart, whose pulse may be

thy praise (emphasis mine).[8]

Not thankful when it pleases me. But a heart whose very pulse sings God's praise.

Do everything without complaining and arguing, so that no one can criticize you. Live clean, innocent lives as children of God, shining like bright lights in a world full of crooked and perverse people.

~ Philippians 2:14–15 NLT

Shine bright in Christ's name.

NOTES

CHAPTER 1

1. A survey on issues related to the body taken by 258 women at Grace Church in Greenville, South Carolina in November 2012.

2. *America The Beautiful*, directed by Darryl Roberts (2007; Chicago, IL: *A Film by Darryl Roberts*, 2008), DVD.

3. Christine Gavin, "8 Ideals of Beauty from Around the World," *Tripbaseblog* (blog), October 14, 2014, http://www.tripbase.com/blog/8-ideals-of-beauty-from-around-the-world/.

4. Cheyenne Ligon, "Beautiful World: Standards of Beauty Around the World," *Her Campus Tulane* (blog), October 14, 2014, http://www.hercampus.com/school/tulane/beautiful-world-standards-beauty-around-world.

CHAPTER 2

1. Chrystie Cole, ed., *Biblical Femininity* (Greenville, SC: Grace Church Publishing, 2013).

2. Lauren F. Winner, *Real Sex* (Grand Rapids, MI: Brazos Press, 2005), 33-34.

3. "3966. meod," Bible Hub, accessed October 14, 2014, http://biblehub.com/hebrew/3966.htm.

4. "2896. towb," Bible Hub, accessed October 14, 2014, http://biblehub.com/hebrew/2896.htm.

5. For more information on this topic, see *Ezer* study *Redeeming Sexuality*.

6. Matthew Lee Anderson, *Earthen Vessels* (Grand Rapids, MI: Bethany House Publishers, 2011), 157.

7. Randy Alcorn, *Heaven* (Carol Stream, IL: Tyndale House Publishers, 2004), 127.

8. Wayne Grudem, "The Creation of Man" in *Systematic Theology* (Grand Rapids, MI: Zondervan), 448.

CHAPTER 3

1. John R. W. Stott, *The Message of the Sermon on the Mount* (Downers Grove, IL: InterVarsity Press, 1978), 157.

2. "573. haplous," Bible Hub, accessed October 14, 2014, http://biblehub.com/greek/573.htm.

3. Stott, 157-158.

4. "Envy," Merriam-Webster, Inc., accessed October 14, 2014, http://www.merriam-webster.com/dictionary/envy.

5. "3788. ophthalmos," Bible Hub, accessed October 14, 2014, http://biblehub.com/greek/3788.htm.

6. "Judgment," Merriam-Webster, Inc., accessed October 14, 2014, http://www.merriam-webster.com/dictionary/judgment.

7. "Discontentment," Merriam-Webster, Inc., accessed October 14, 2014, http://www.merriam-webster.com/dictionary/discontent.

8. "Entitlement," Merriam-Webster, Inc., accessed October 14, 2014, http://www.merriam-webster.com/dictionary/entitlement.

CHAPTER 4

1. "Narcissism," Dictonary.com, LCC, accessed September 20, 2014, http://dictionary.reference.com/browse/narcissism.

2. Tim Keller, Introduction to *Counterfeit Gods* (New York: Penguin Group, 2009), xvii - xviii.

3. "Lupita Nyongo Delivers Moving 'Black Women Hollywood' Acceptance Speech," *Essence,* February 28, 2014, accessed October 14, 2014, http://www.essence.com/2014/02/27/lupita-nyongo-delivers-moving-black-women-hollywood-acceptance-speech/.

4. Tim Keller, "Reading 2.2 Idols of the Heart," in *The Gospel and the Heart* (Fellows Intensive, 2008), http://www.scribd.com/doc/50551002/0410-001-Tim-Keller-pdf.

5. Melissa Stranger, "Attractive People Are More Successful," *Business Insider,* October 9, 2012, accessed October 14, 2014, http://www.businessinsider.com/attractive-people-are-more-successful-2012-9.

6. Blaise Pascal, *Pascal's Pensées* (New York: E.P. Dutton & Co., 1958), 114.

7. For more on the freedom of self-forgetfulness, see *The Freedom of Self-Forgetfulness* by Tim Keller.

CHAPTER 5

1. Gordon D. Fee, *The First Epistle to the Corinthians* (Grand Rapids, MI: Eerdmans Publishing, 1987), 257.

2. Thomas Edward McComiskey ed., *The Minor Prophets* (Grand Rapids, MI: Baker Book House, 1998), 976-977.

3. For more on this concept see the Ezer study *Redeeming Sexuality.*

4. Marva J. Dawn, *Truly the Community* (Grand Rapids, MI: Eerdmans, 1992), 77-79.

5. Ben Patterson, "The Goodness of Sex and the Glory of God" in *Sex and the Supremacy of Christ,* ed. John Piper and Justin Taylor (Wheaton, IL: Crossway, 2005), 57.

6. Cole, *Biblical Femininity,* 25.

7. See additional resources page for suggested resources on spiritual disciplines.

8. Mike Cosper, "Grace-Motivated Dieting," *The Gospel Coalition*, January 15, 2012, accessed October 14, 2014, http://www.thegospelcoalition.org/article/grace-motivated-dieting/.

9. "Importance of Sleep : Six reasons not to scrimp on sleep," *Harvard Health Publications,* January 2009, accessed October 14, 2014, http://www.health.harvard.edu/press_releases/importance_of_sleep_and_health.

10. Louann Brizendine, *The Female Brain* (New York: Three Rivers Press, 2006), 37.

11. "The Benefits of Physical Activity," *The Nutrition Source,* Harvard School of Public Health, accessed October 14, 2014, http://www.hsph.harvard.edu/nutritionsource/staying-active-full-story/.

12. "Exercise: 7 benefits of regular physical activity," *The Mayo Clinic*, accessed October 14, 2014, http://www.mayoclinic.org/healthy-living/fitness/in-depth/exercise/art-20048389?pg=1.

13. John Dunlop, *Wellness to the Glory of God* (Wheaton, IL: Crossway, 2014), 34.

14. "How much physical activity do adults need?," *Centers for Disease Control and Prevention*, accessed October 14, 2014, http://www.cdc.gov/physicalactivity/everyone/guidelines/adults.html.

CHAPTER 6

1. Fyodor Dostoyevsky, "The Confession of a Passionate Heart - In Verse" in *The Brothers Karamazov* (Christian Classics Ethereal Library), accessed October 14, 2014, http://www.ccel.org/ccel/dostoevsky/brothers.iii_3.html.

CHAPTER 7

1. C. H. Spurgeon, "A Bed and Its Covering," *The Spurgeon*

Archive (delivered at New Park Street Chapel, Southwark, January 9, 1859) accessed October 14, 2014, http://www.spurgeon.org/sermons/0244.htm.

2. R. Kent Hughes, *Colossians and Philemon: The Supremacy of Christ* (Wheaton, IL: Crossway, 1989), 64.

3. Dennis Kinlaw, "November 14: Subtle Calls to Sin" in *This Day with the Master* (Grand Rapids, MI: Zondervan, 2002).

4. "Grumble", Bible Hub, accessed October 14, 2014, http://biblehub.com/concordance/g/grumble.htm.

5. Jerry Bridges, *The Practice of Godliness* (Colorado Springs, CO: NavPress, 1996), 86.

6. Paige Benton Brown, "Kingdom Matters" (presented at The Gospel Coalition National Women's Conference, Orlando, Florida, June 21-24, 2012) http://resources.thegospelcoalition.org/library/kingdom-matters.

7. Dale Ralph Davis, *1 Samuel, Looking on the Heart* (Ross-shire, Great Britain: Christian Focus Publications, 2003), 77.

8. George Herbert, "Gratefulnesse" in *The Temple* (Christian Classics Ethereal Library) accessed October 14, 2014, http://www.ccel.org/h/herbert/temple/Gratefulnesse.html.

ADDITIONAL RESOURCES

RESOURCES RELATED TO SPIRITUAL DISCIPLINES:
Prayer by Paul Miller
The Rest of God by Mark Buchanan
Spiritual Disciplines in the Christian Life by Donald S. Whitney

Body Matters is an *Ezer* resource from Grace Church. The *Ezer* ministry exists to make mature disciples by equipping women to live a life of faith and follow Jesus in all areas of their lives. For studies on other issues pertaining to women, such as *Biblical Femininity* and *Redeeming Sexuality,* go to gracechurchsc.org.

For corresponding videos, articles, and downloads, go to gracechurchsc.org/ministries/women/body-matters/.

Our corresponding studies for men are *Quest for Authentic Manhood, Quest for Purity, A Man and His Wife, A Man and His Son, A Man and His Daughter,* and *A Man and His Work.*

For more information on these, please visit gracechurchsc.org.

For more information about

Body Matters

please visit:

www.gracechurchsc.org
info@gracechurchsc.org
www.facebook.com/gracechurchezer

For more information about
AMBASSADOR INTERNATIONAL
please visit:

www.ambassador-international.com
@AmbassadorIntl
www.facebook.com/AmbassadorIntl

Also by **Chrystie Cole** and **Grace Church**

Biblical Femininity
*Discovering Clarity and Freedom in
God's Design for Women*

&

Redeeming Sexuality
*Exploring God's Design for
Sex and Sexuality*

available through Grace Church
gracechurchsc.org